SPIRITUALITY IS EXTREMELY DANGEROUS. WHY?

SPIRITUALITY IS EXTREMELY DANGEROUS. WHY?

A Walkover from Mindnullness to Mindfulness

BEAUGRUN

An Introductory Volume
of the Beaugrun School of Thoughts

Beaugrun Publications

Beaugrun Books

published by Beaugrun Publications

Category: Observational Studies of the Spirit World

'Let us Crack All Odds!' — Series Book I

SPIRITUALITY IS EXTREMELY DANGEROUS. WHY?

First published in India, 2026

ISBN: **978-93-341-8859-2**

Layout and Design: Beaugrun Communications
Typeset in: Garamond
Printed in India

Published by:

Beaugrun Publications

Registered Office: 04-270B, Beaugrun Towers, Neericode P.O., Alangad, Aluva 683511, Kerala, India

Correspondence: P.B. No. 16, Aluva, Kochi 683501, Kerala, India

Email: **beaugrunpublications@gmail.com**
Website: www.beaugrun.com

Disclaimer:

The views, opinions, and findings expressed in this book are entirely the author's own, drawn from three decades of personal observational research. They do not represent the views of the publisher. The facts presented have been verified to the extent possible, and neither the author nor the publisher shall be held responsible for any errors or omissions.

This work reflects the author's original observational research and intellectual contribution. AI writing tools were used in the preparation of this manuscript. The core ideas, experiences, and conclusions remain solely those of the author.

Foreign Rights & Translation Inquiries:

Beaugrun Publications welcomes inquiries from foreign publishers and translators interested in producing editions of this work in other languages. The author retains all translation, foreign-edition, audio, and dramatic rights. Inquiries may be directed to the publisher at the address or email above.

DEDICATION

To every soul who ever heard a whisper from beyond —

and wondered if it was real.

It was.

In search of the mystery behind the thought process.

For every disturbance, there may have an unknown reason.
We have to search.

Be alert in mind. Test every thought.

A Note to the Reader

• • •

This book is a sincere offering of one observer's personal perspectives — drawn from three decades of quiet watching, listening, and reflection. It is not a prescription. It is not a universal conclusion. It is an honest sharing of what was observed.

Where these observations align with scripture — it is noted. Where they differ from established science or theology — they are presented clearly as the author's personal perspective alone.

• • •

Some chapters of this book touch sensitive territory — grief, loss, unexplained experiences, the realm of Spirits.

If at any point while reading you feel distressed, disturbed, or overwhelmed — *please pause.*

Speak with a trusted mentor, your family doctor, or a qualified therapist.

These experiences deserve proper human support — not silence.

This book is not a substitute for professional guidance. It is an invitation to honest reflection.

• • •

Read with an open mind. Analyse with your own experience.

And always — listen to your heart.

A Word Before You Begin

• • •

This book was not planned. It was observed.

It began not with a pen, but with a pressing need to share observations I had never encountered in any book I read.

Three decades of watching. Listening. Questioning what others accepted without question. Sitting with people in grief, in restlessness, in confusion — people who experienced things they could not easily explain and were often told to ignore them.

I could not ignore them.

Over those decades, I watched people struggle with burdens they could not name. Emotions without clear origin. Words that seemed to arrive uninvited. Presences felt, though unseen.

I am not a theologian. I am not a psychologist. I am an observer — sincere, persistent, and at times restless — who could not accept that such experiences carried no meaning.

Psychology warned that such pursuits may lead to illusion, delusion, or misinterpretation. I heard that warning. *I did not stop.*

Because what I observed could not be dismissed so easily.

This work moves across familiar territories — religion, psychology, and science — yet pauses where explanations often remain incomplete. It borrows from each, and goes where none, on its own, has fully gone.

Consider a disciplined approach to inquiry — one that examines truth and falsehood with care, weighing words, claims, and evidence. And yet, even within such discipline, what appears true to one may be contested by another. Still, there remains an underlying reality that calls for deeper examination.

Much about the human mind remains under study. Even where knowledge exists, it continues to be questioned, refined, and expanded.

In such a landscape, it may be useful to ask not only what is known, but what remains unexplored.

• • •

Across traditions, cultures, and scholarly works, there appears a recurring suggestion — that human experience may not always be self-contained. *Something* influences, shapes, and moves human beings, yet this possibility is often softened, redirected, or left unexplored.

My search was simple. *What is this influence? Where does it arise?*

At times, I observed experiences that seemed to affect consciousness in subtle but noticeable ways — moments of disturbance, lack of clarity, or inner disquiet. For clarity, I came to describe such states as *mindnullness.*

Alongside these, I also observed moments of relief, clarity, and steadiness — states that may be described as *mindfulness.*

The movement between these states, and the question of how such clarity may be sustained, became part of my inquiry.

Over time, it became evident that these observations were rarely addressed in a direct and accessible way. The need to share them grew — not as a conclusion, but as an invitation.

And if something moves a human being from within, can it truly be without form, direction, or meaning?

• • •

Every reader begins with a position.

Some approach with belief. Some with doubt. Some remain undecided.

These positions are shaped over time — by experience, learning, and interpretation. *What we believe shapes how we perceive. What we experience shapes what we come to believe.*

Yet a question remains.

Do we hold our beliefs — or do they begin to shape us before we are fully aware?

And if beliefs shape us — what stands behind them?

Let us observe.

• • •

Doubt often initiates thought. Thought shapes feeling. Feeling may influence response.

What may require attention is *how* these processes unfold — and *what* influences them.

Some of what follows may appear unfamiliar. It is not presented to conclude, but to be examined.

• • •

This work does not begin with belief. *It begins with experience.*

The perspectives presented here arise from long observation and reflection. They are offered not to compel agreement, but to invite examination.

Before you proceed, consider:

Have you ever felt something you could not fully explain?

Have you experienced a thought or feeling that seemed to arrive without clear origin?

Have you noticed moments of clarity — and moments where it seemed to fade?

If these questions feel familiar, then *you are not beginning without experience.*

Read with attention. Pause where needed. Keep what clarifies. Question what remains.

A detailed table of contents appears at the end of the book.

This work does not attempt to present everything at once. It introduces what can be observed and allows understanding to develop as the journey continues.

What you hold is not a final answer. *It is an honest journey.*

Read with an open heart.

— *Beaugrun*

Acknowledgements

• • •

To every person who shared their experience openly and without fear — *you are the foundation of this work.*

To my family, for their patience and support.

To the grieving, the questioning, the quietly searching — *this book exists because of you.*

To the pioneers and visionaries of Artificial Intelligence — and to the AI systems their work made possible, which served as thinking partners through many long conversations during the shaping of this book, helping bring my observations and reflections into a form that could be shared with the reader.

And above all — *gratitude to God.*

Not from the mouth. From the heart.

Contents

A Note to the Reader

A Word Before You Begin

Acknowledgements

Why I Write — A Note from the Author

PART I — Foundations of Thought and Spirit

1. Thinking — A Conversation with Spirits
2. If Brain Has No Memory, Mind Has No Power, And Body Has No Life
3. Let Us Do Some Chemistry of Spirits
4. A Walkover from Mindnullness to Mindfulness

PART II — Diagnostics of Disturbance

5. Curtail Feelings Before Emotions Conquer Behaviour
6. The Body Speaks Before the Mind Names
7. Memory Loss and Forgetfulness — A Chemical Analysing
8. Hurt Not Others. It Returns. The Boomerang Effect

PART III — Discernment and Environment

9. Are Natural Disasters Preplanned? Animals Discern.
10. Spiritual and Intellectual Protection
11. Why Certain Places Disturb Us
12. Why Powerful Words Clear What Advice Cannot Move

PART IV — Capacity, Talent, Innocence

13. Are Talents and Skills Biological or Spiritual?
14. Innocence Teaches Perception Better Than Science

Afterword

A Few Words to Carry

A Questionnaire for Self-Reflection

The Series Ahead — Why the Need of the Hour

Glossary of Beaugrun Terms

About the Author

A detailed table of contents appears at the end of the book.

Why I Write

Three Decades of Observation into the Spirit Kingdom

• • •

This book does not emerge from a university. It does not carry institutional endorsement. It is not the product of a funded research programme or a peer-reviewed academic exercise.

It emerges from something less comfortable — and arguably more honest. *Three decades of direct, persistent, and careful observation of human behaviour through the lens of spirit influence.*

I am a lawyer by profession. My work has required the careful examination of evidence, the identification of inconsistencies, and the construction of arguments that can withstand scrutiny. That discipline has shaped every observation recorded in this work.

But the observations themselves began long before the legal training. They began with questions that conventional frameworks — religious, scientific, psychological — consistently failed to answer satisfactorily.

Why does a person behave in ways that contradict their own stated values — repeatedly, inexplicably, against their own interests?

Why do thoughts arrive unbidden — fully formed, uninvited, and sometimes entirely foreign to the person receiving them?

Why does fear arise in safe environments without identifiable cause?

How does sleeplessness appear in a peaceful ambience — where one enjoys sound sleep, while the other lies disturbed?

Why has no neuroscientist, despite decades of sophisticated research, located a single cell or precise region where memory is stored?

Why have even eminent scholars — those bound by calling to light the path — retreated into comfortable euphemisms like *"mystery," "myth,"* or *"phenomenon"?* Words that neither explain nor illuminate, but quietly turn away the reader who hungers for fact and truth.

These are not rhetorical questions. They are honest observations that mainstream frameworks have not resolved — merely renamed, reframed, or quietly moved past.

Dr. Karl Spencer Lashley spent decades searching for the physical location of memory in the human brain. He never found it. That finding was significant. The field largely absorbed it without honest resolution.

I noticed. And kept noticing.

Across three decades, the observations accumulated — patterns of human behaviour, experience, and suffering that pointed consistently toward something operating beyond conventional biological and psychological explanation. Not supernatural in the sensational sense. But genuinely beyond what current frameworks honestly account for.

This book is an attempt to present those observations — carefully, precisely, and within their honest limits.

It does not demand belief. It presents a framework — the foundational principles of the *Beaugrun School of Thoughts* — as an honest invitation to examine what mainstream thinking has left genuinely unresolved, weighing the evidence and placing both possibilities before the reader, as in a matter laid before a jury.

I withdrew from nearly a decade of legal practice to develop and ground these ideas. That was not a casual decision. It was made because the observations demanded serious attention — and that attention demanded significant time.

What follows is the result of that time.

• • •

A word of honest caution before you proceed.

This book will challenge assumptions. It will question frameworks you may hold with considerable confidence — scientific, religious, philosophical, psychological.

That challenge is offered with genuine respect for those frameworks and the brilliant minds that built them. *Even prominent thinkers make errors. Even established frameworks have honest limitations.* Identifying those limitations is not disrespect. It is the necessary work of honest inquiry.

As I hold — good and bad are set before you. The choice remains yours.

These observations and findings are placed before you.

The choice to discern remains yours.

Let us not conclude too quickly but observe what may be working behind the mind.

Read what follows with the same honest and open scrutiny I have applied across three decades of observation.

That is all that is asked.

— *Beaugrun*

Founder, Beaugrun School of Thoughts
2026

PART I

Foundations of Thought and Spirit

The Metaphysical Ground on Which the Discerning Life Begins

1. Thinking — A Conversation with Spirits

2. If Brain Has No Memory, Mind Has No Power,
And Body Has No Life, How Does a Human Function?

3. Let Us Do Some Chemistry of Spirits

4. A Walkover from Mindnullness to Mindfulness

CHAPTER ONE

Thinking — Conversation with Spirits

Have you ever heard the voice of a loved one — long gone — suddenly speak in your mind? Their exact words. Their tone. As if they never left.

Suddenly, you feel it. That wave of nostalgia. You glance behind you, beside you — sensing a presence.

Someone nearby.

Unseen.

There you are.

Relax.

Every journey starts with a leap.

We are getting ready to delve into the Kingdom of Spirits.

Welcome to the Kingdom of Spirits.

A new perspective. A new understanding.

Not to believe. Not to reject. But to observe.

Let us walk gently.

The human body is simply a carrier — and Spirits are Words.

> *"It is the Spirit that gives life, not the flesh. The words I have spoken to you are Spirit."*
>
> — John 6:63

Those words you heard. That voice you remembered. It is not mystical. It is not illusion. It is real. Psychology may call it psychotic.

Parapsychology may offer another name. But the truth is simpler — in that moment, you either gained or lost energy. Something was exchanged.

And in that moment, something stirs.

Some feel it as a quiet anointing — a warmth, a settling, as though something sacred has gently touched them. Others are moved to tears, without quite knowing why. And then there are those gripped by fear — a sudden, nameless dread that follows them into the night, robbing them of sleep.

The heart tightens. A pressure, unexplained, sits heavy on the chest. The blood runs faster. A heightened alertness takes over — every small sound in the room becomes sharp, startling, threatening. The creak of a floorboard. The hum of silence itself.

Some shake it off. They move on, and the moment fades like a dream by morning.

But for others — it does not fade. It follows. It lingers in the corners of rooms, in the stillness before sleep, in the echo of familiar voices.

So, the question must be asked — were those experiences real, or were they not?

• • •

Opening the Pandora's Box of the Spirit World

Most of us grew up hearing the word *Spirit* and quietly filing it under one of two categories:

Religion. Or myth.

And perhaps that made life simpler. Tidier. More manageable.

But here we are — together — about to do something quietly radical.

We are going to open the box.

Not to frighten. Not to compel. Not to tell you what to believe or discard what you already hold.

Simply — to look inside. Together.

Believe it or not, that choice remains entirely yours. It will remain yours on every page that follows.

But consider this before we begin.

When something happens upon your body — a sudden heaviness in the chest, a warmth with no source, a presence felt in an empty room, a fear that arrives before any visible threat — that is not a theory.

That is an experience.

Experiences are felt.

They happen live — upon the body, in real time.

You felt it. Whatever it was.

Now — what was it?

Science may describe such moments as chemical activity — and that may be so.

But we are not only asking what happened. We are asking how and why it arose in that moment.

What moved the body to respond so instantly?

What set those reactions into motion?

We laugh at some words and remain untouched by others.

We feel drawn to certain moments and unsettled by others.

If the response is chemical — what guides the response?

Let us stay with the experience a little longer.

Observe your experience.

At times, a sense of ease may follow.

It can feel as though something has loosened — within the body, within the mind.

This is often described as *mindfulness*.

We will return to this.

What settles, and what disturbs? What allows clarity — and what obscures it?

We will look more closely at what may be called *mindnullness*, and how, at times, it gives way to *mindfulness*.

And perhaps more importantly — why this shift does not occur for everyone in the same way.

For now, let us not rush ahead.

Let us observe — just a little longer.

That act of pausing — of comparing what you felt with what you know, of sitting with the question honestly rather than rushing to dismiss or explain —

That is *discernment*.

Every living being has a limited ability to discern.

And discernment is simply learning — in its most honest form.

Some will call what we explore here *myth*.

But consider what myth is.

Myth is not falsehood. It is the word we reach for when something is too real to dismiss — and too unfamiliar to explain.

It is confusion wearing a confident mask.

It says: *This may be real. But I cannot explain it. And what I cannot explain — I will call myth.*

Fair enough.

Then let us explore the heart of myths — together.

Because at the heart of every myth, something true has always been waiting.

Is it a force — or is it a spirit?

Is it a force with a shape — or is it a shape-forming energy?

If it has form, it must be named.

Here, the term *Spirit* is used for a force that takes form.

• • •

It's Different

Before we go further into the Kingdom of Spirits, we must first pause and ask a question that most books never ask.

What is *thinking*?

Not what a thought is *about* — but what the act of thinking itself is. Who does it. Where it lives. How far it reaches.

Do animals think the way we do?

And what of creatures with no brain and no heart — what could *their* thinking be like?

We cannot know fully. We can only wonder.

But wondering itself is a kind of thinking — and perhaps the most honest kind.

Because if we are to speak of spirits — of voices heard in the mind, of presences felt in empty rooms, of conversations held with those no longer here — then we must first widen what we mean by *thought.*

We have been taught, most of us, that thinking is what the human brain does. A private theatre inside the skull. A silent voice speaking in our own language. Something that belongs to us.

But life suggests a different story.

And that story begins in the most unexpected places.

• • •

The Thinkers Without a Brain

Consider the slime mould.

It is not a plant. Not an animal. Not a fungus. A single, giant cell — with many nuclei, no brain, no nervous system, no heart.

And yet —

A researcher once placed oat flakes on a map of Tokyo, marking the city's major railway stations. A slime mould was released at the centre. Within a day, it formed a network connecting all the food sources — closely resembling the actual Tokyo rail system, designed by human engineers over decades.

A creature with no brain had solved a complex spatial problem.

Consider the jellyfish.

No brain. No heart. Only a diffuse network of nerves.

And yet the box jellyfish navigates around obstacles, hunts, and avoids danger.

Something in it perceives. Something in it responds.

Consider the sea sponge.

Among the most ancient life forms on Earth.

No neurons. No brain. No heart.

And yet it coordinates thousands of cells in a unified function.

Scientists have found that it carries the genetic precursors of synapses — the very machinery associated with thought — long before brains existed.

The seed of mind appears before the structure of mind.

Consider the plant.

No brain. No heart.

Yet the mimosa leaf learns. Repeated gentle touches, without harm, and it stops closing. A form of memory.

Trees communicate through airborne signals. Roots interact with fungi in complex exchanges — trading nutrients in systems older than human civilisation.

Sunflowers anticipate sunrise — turning east before dawn.

Anticipation suggests pattern recognition. And pattern recognition suggests a form of thinking.

Consider the single cell.

A paramecium — microscopic, without nerves or a brain. Yet it moves toward nourishment and away from harm.

It adapts.

Life responds — everywhere.

With a brain or without.

• • •

Then What Is the Brain For?

If organisms without brains can respond, adapt, and organise — what then is the role of the brain?

What is the role of the heart?

Perhaps this:

The brain and the heart are not the origin of life or thought. They are *amplifiers.*

Life appears to sense and respond long before these structures evolved.

The brain enables scale — coordinating vast complexity. The heart enables circulation — sustaining a larger system.

The human being, then, is not the first thinker — but a more complex one.

A slime mould responds within its limits.

A human reflects across time, imagines, records, communicates.

Nikola Tesla, the man who lit the modern world, said this himself in plain words. *"My brain is only a receiver,"* he wrote. *"In the universe there is a core from which we obtain knowledge, strength and inspiration."* He was not being mystical. He was being honest. A man who had given humanity alternating current was telling us, plainly, that he was not the source of his ideas — only their landing strip.

And the body, on rare occasion, has confirmed this in startling ways. In 1980, the British neurologist John Lorber published a paper in *Science* magazine with a title that unsettled his profession: *Is Your Brain Really*

Necessary? He had scanned a young Sheffield mathematics student with an IQ of 126 and a first-class honours degree — and found that the boy's skull was almost entirely filled with cerebrospinal fluid. The brain itself was a sheet barely a millimetre thick, lining the inside of the skull. The boy was, by every measurable standard, perfectly fine. Lorber went on to find dozens like him.

If thinking is what the brain *does*, how does the man with almost no brain still think?

This raises a question:

If thinking is not confined to the brain —

does it begin there at all?

Or does it pass *through* it?

Perhaps the brain is not a factory.

Perhaps it is an interface.

An instrument.

And if thinking is not produced within it —

then where does it arise?

Here, inquiry deepens.

And science, for now, grows quiet.

• • •

The Footprints of Thoughts

Science can tell us, with great precision, what happens in the brain when a thought arrives. Chemicals are released at the gaps between neurons — glutamate, dopamine, serotonin, and many others. Hormones flow. Patterns of electricity ripple across vast networks of cells. All of this can be measured.

But here is the strangeness science has uncovered and rarely tells the public.

In the nineteen-eighties, a researcher named Benjamin Libet made a discovery that unsettled the scientific world. He showed that the brain begins preparing to act *before* the person is aware of deciding to act. By almost half a second. Later experiments pushed this gap wider still.

The decision happens first. The awareness of the decision comes afterward.

This suggests that the chemicals in the brain may not be the *origin* of the thought, but a *response* to it. Like steam rising from something already heated. The true thought arrives from somewhere deeper, somewhere faster, somewhere science cannot yet find. And the brain, with all its chemistry, is busy translating that arrival into a form the body can use.

The chemicals are footprints.

But who is the walker?

• • •

The Spirit in the Particle

Let us follow the question all the way down.

When human life begins — at the union of two cells in the womb — there is no visible life. Only molecules. Only atoms. Only the tiny particles that physics has spent a century trying to understand. And yet from that invisible beginning, a living, thinking, loving being emerges.

Where did life come from?

It was not added later, like salt to a dish. It must have been present already — somehow, somewhere — in the particles themselves.

And this is where modern physics begins to whisper things the ancient traditions always said aloud.

The particles that make up your body are not dead little marbles. Quantum physics suggests they exist in clouds of possibility until observed. They respond to each other across great distances in ways no signal can explain — what Einstein himself called, in discomfort, *spooky action at a distance.* Thousands of experiments have confirmed it. The particle is not a thing. The particle is a participant.

In recent thought, some of the most serious philosophers of our time have begun to say openly what the mystics said long ago — that consciousness, or the seed of it, must be present at every level of matter. Because if awareness is not in the particle in some form, how does it appear in the brain, which is only arranged matter? You cannot squeeze water from stone. If thinking is in us, it must have been in what we are made of.

The Upanishads said this thousands of years ago. The Sufi mystics said it. Indigenous elders across every continent said it. That stone is alive. That river has a spirit. That the breath of the Divine is in every atom.

At the same time, science has not yet confirmed this.

But science has opened the door.

And through that door, a very old understanding is walking back into the room.

• • •

The Narrow Window

Consider something few of us have ever paused to consider.

The human ear hears only roughly twenty cycles per second to twenty thousand. Below that, and above it, there is sound — vast oceans of it — that we will never hear. The elephant speaks in frequencies too low for us. The bat and the dolphin speak in frequencies too high. A dog hears a whistle we cannot. A moth hears the sonar of its hunter, silent to us.

Who decided that the human would hear only this narrow window? Not us. We did not choose our own ears. We were given them. And we have mistaken the small band we *can* hear for the whole of what is being spoken.

The same is true of sight. We see only a sliver of the light that fills the universe. Infrared and ultraviolet move past our eyes unseen. A bee sees patterns on a flower we cannot. A snake sees the heat of a living body glowing in the dark. What we call *visible* is only visible to us.

Now ask the honest question.

If there are beings elsewhere — on other worlds, in other dimensions, in forms we cannot yet imagine — would they speak in our frequencies? Would they see in our colours? Or would they communicate in bands of sound, of light, of something else entirely, that our senses were never tuned to receive?

And what of the spirits? If a voice is speaking in a frequency the ear was never built to catch, where does that voice go? Perhaps it will find another door. Perhaps it enters not through the ear, but through the mind itself — arriving as thought rather than sound. A loved one's words, long gone, suddenly speaking from within.

Science is already beginning to search for such things. Researchers scan the skies for signals from other civilisations, turning their instruments to frequencies far beyond human hearing. They assume — reasonably — that if life exists elsewhere, it will not speak in the narrow band we were given. They are learning to listen past the ear.

Every signal has a source. What we do not hear may not be absent — only beyond the range we have learned to detect.

And so must we. If we wish to hear what is truly being spoken, we must stop assuming that the small window of our senses is the whole of the room.

• • •

The Chain Unbroken

So let us see what we now hold.

The brainless creature thinks — because thought was already in its cells.

The cells think — because thought was already in the molecules that built them.

The molecules carry life — because life was already in the atoms.

The atoms carry a whisper of something — because spirit was already in the particles.

And so, the human being is not the inventor of thought. Human beings are the most elaborate *receiver* of it. A radio tuned finely to a broadcast that has been filling the universe since before the stars were lit.

But the radio is narrow. It catches only a small part of what is being broadcast. The rest passes through us, unheard and unseen, touching us in ways we cannot name — as warmth, as dread, as the sudden voice of one long gone.

• • •

The Field You Are Standing In

So let us return to where we began.

To the voice of the loved one, long gone, suddenly speaking in your mind. To the presence felt beside you in an empty room. To the warmth with no source. To the dread that arrived before any visible threat.

Many have been troubled by such moments — and not all of them ordinary people. Mark Twain, known to the world as a great humorist but in private a man marked all his life by what he had seen, recorded in his autobiography a dream he had as a young Mississippi steamboat pilot in the spring of 1858. He saw his beloved younger brother Henry lying in a metal coffin balanced on two chairs in a parlour, a bouquet of white flowers on his chest, with a single crimson rose at the centre. Twain woke deeply shaken. Two weeks later, the steamboat *Pennsylvania* exploded on the river, and Henry was killed. When Twain reached Memphis, he was led to where the dead lay. Most rested in plain wooden coffins. Henry alone — because the local women had been moved by his youth — lay in a metal one, balanced on two chairs in a parlour. As Twain stood there, a woman entered and laid a bouquet on his brother's chest. White flowers. A single crimson rose at the centre.

Twain never claimed to understand what he had seen. He simply said, for the rest of his life, that he had seen it.

You have now walked a small distance. You have seen that the creature without a brain still thinks. That the brain itself is not a factory of thought but an antenna. That thought may arrive before the chemicals that carry it. That the particles of your body are not dead things, but participants in something vast. That your senses catch only a narrow band of what is being broadcast — in sound, in light, and perhaps in thought as well.

You carry this now. Even if you set the book down.

And the voice you heard — the presence you felt — begins to look less like illusion and more like a signal. One among many. Perhaps reaching you through a door your ordinary senses were not built to guard.

And if thought can arrive from beyond the self — then not every impulse, not every error, may fully belong to the one who experiences it.

Could it be, then, that what we call *error* is not entirely human?

This is not yet a conclusion.

But it is a question worth holding.

Does this mean that every unusual feeling must be examined with care?

Sometimes, what appears as a signal may be unclear, and the mind itself may go out of order — what medicine would call a disturbance of the psyche and treat as illness. That too deserves care, not interpretation.

Discernment, as we spoke of earlier, is the precautionary work to be practised — not to accept everything, and not to dismiss everything, but to learn the difference.

Some experiences are memories. And yet — what if memory itself does not live in the brain, but arrives from somewhere? Karl Lashley, a scientist, spent thirty-three years cutting into brains to find where a single memory is stored. He never found it. Perhaps he was not wrong. Perhaps he was simply looking in the wrong place. Perhaps memory is not a record kept in flesh, but a moving energy — an associated spirit — returning to us repeatedly. This may be why the same memory haunts one person and entertains another. The memory is the same. But the spirit within it meets each soul differently.

Some experiences are simple fatigue. Some are the body speaking in its own language. But some — *some* — are real arrivals, from somewhere the instruments of science have not yet learned to measure.

The Kingdom of Spirits is not a place far away. It is not above the clouds, nor below the ground. It is not reached by ritual or earned by worthiness.

It is among us.

It is the field you are already standing in. You have been standing in it all your life. You were simply not told its name.

And now, perhaps, you are noticing.

In the chapters ahead, we will walk further into this field together. We will ask where thoughts come from, and why they clothe themselves in words. We will ask why so much of the truth has been hidden from us through the centuries. We will listen to voices that were silenced and find that their silenced truths still speak — if we lean close.

For now, let what has been said settle.

And the next time a voice speaks in your mind, or a presence brushes past you in an empty room — do not rush to dismiss, and do not rush to name.

Simply pause.

Listen.

And remember — you are not alone in what you experience.

• • •

Thinking is a form of inner conversation.

Thoughts are words. They carry direction — some steady, some disturb.

Notice which thoughts appear before your unrest begins.

CHAPTER TWO

If Brain Has No Memory, Mind Has No Power, And Body Has No Life — How Does a Human Function?

If Lashley spent decades searching for memory in the brain
and never found it,
the honest question is not how memory hides.

The honest question is whether memory was ever there to find.

• • •

Why the Silence

In 1929, the American psychologist Karl Spencer Lashley published a paper that should have rearranged the foundations of neuroscience and did not.

Lashley had spent years training rats to run mazes. The training was painstaking. The rats learned the routes. Their performance could be measured. Then Lashley began doing something the surrounding scientific culture found unsettling. He surgically removed portions of the rats' brains, in different locations and different sizes, to find where the memory of the maze was stored.

He could not find it.

No matter where he cut, the rats retained their memory of the maze. The performance degraded with the *amount* of brain tissue removed, but it degraded uniformly regardless of *which* part of the brain had been damaged. The memory was not in any location. It seemed to be everywhere, and therefore, on any straightforward reading of where memories should be stored, it was nowhere.

Lashley named the phenomenon *mass action.* The brain, he proposed, stored memory through some property of the whole that was not reducible to any of its parts. He published. The paper was read. The field absorbed the result without honest resolution and moved on.

The silence that followed was the field's answer.

• • •

The Fog That Will Not Lift

Almost a century has passed since Lashley's paper. The search for the location of memory has continued, with progressively more sophisticated tools. Functional MRI. Optogenetics. Single-cell recording. The mapping of neural circuits in unprecedented detail. The Human Connectome Project. The Brain Initiative. Billions of dollars. Tens of thousands of papers.

The location of memory has not been found.

This is not because the search has been incompetent. The search has been brilliant. The brilliance has not yielded the discovery, because the discovery is not there to be made by this method. The location of memory is not in the brain in the sense that the search has assumed.

The field knows this, in some part of itself. The honest researchers, in private, will admit it. The research papers continue, year after year, with the same caveats. *We have not yet found the precise mechanism. Further research is needed. The complexity of the brain is greater than we had anticipated.* These caveats have been the standard closing paragraphs of memory papers for a century.

The most striking confirmation of Lashley's finding came, slowly and against his own expectation, from a man who had begun his career convinced that memory could be located. Wilder Penfield, the Canadian neurosurgeon and founder of the Montreal Neurological Institute, conducted thousands of operations on conscious epilepsy patients through the 1940s and 1950s. With the skull open and the brain exposed, he would touch electrical probes to specific points on the cortex and ask the patient — fully awake — what they experienced. The patients reported vivid memories: a song heard in childhood, the smell of a mother's kitchen, a long-forgotten conversation. Each touch on the same spot produced the same memory. For two decades, Penfield was certain he was mapping the storage sites of memory itself.

Then, late in his career, he stopped.

In his final book, *The Mystery of the Mind*, published in 1975, Penfield wrote that he had been wrong. The cortical points he had stimulated were not *storing* the memories. They were *doors* — gateways through which memories returned from somewhere else. The memories themselves, he had come to believe, were not in the tissue at all. The most extensively documented brain-mapping in the history of neuroscience had brought its author, against his own initial conviction, to the same conclusion as Lashley.

> *"For my own part, after years of striving to explain the mind on the basis of brain-action alone, I have come to the conclusion that it is simpler if one adopts the hypothesis that our being does consist of two fundamental elements."*
>
> — Wilder Penfield, *The Mystery of the Mind*

The neurosurgeon had become, by the end of his life, something close to a mystic. Not by faith. By data.

The fog will not lift, because the fog is not fog. The fog is the absence of what was being looked for in the place where the looking was being done.

• • •

Let Us Crack the Iceberg of Mind

The question this book is willing to ask is the question the field has been declining to ask. *If memory is not in the brain, where is it?*

The proposition is that memory is in the field — the same field the previous chapter described as full of operating forces, the same field in which thinking arrives as report from beyond the brain. *Memory is not stored. Memory is accessed.* The brain docs not contain memory. The brain reaches into the field and retrieves what is held there.

This is consistent with the data Lashley produced. If memory were stored locally, removing the location should remove the memory. Lashley found this did not happen. If memory is held in the field and the brain accesses the field, removing parts of the brain should degrade access without erasing what is being accessed. This is what Lashley found. The data fits the field-access model. The data does not fit the local-storage model.

The proposition is also consistent with experiences that the local-storage model cannot accommodate. Patients who have lost large portions of brain tissue retaining detailed memories of events that occurred before the loss. People in deep meditation accessing memories they had no conscious access to before. People near death reporting memories from earliest childhood, before the brain regions associated with those memories had developed sufficiently to encode them. Twin studies in which one twin remembers what the other has experienced, without the experience having been communicatcd. Each of thcsc is anomalous under the local-storage model. None is anomalous under the field-access model.

There is one further piece of evidence the field-access model accommodates and the local-storage model cannot. In 1953, a young man named Henry Molaison underwent brain surgery to cure his epilepsy. The surgeon removed his hippocampus on both sides — a region by then thought to be essential to memory. The surgery cured the seizures. It also did something the surgeon had not anticipated. From that moment until his death fifty-five years later, Henry could not form a single new conscious memory. Every morning he met his doctors as if for the first time.

And yet — and this is the strange part the textbooks rarely linger on — Henry could still *learn*. Given a mirror-drawing task day after day, he became measurably better at it, even though he did not remember having attempted it before. He could still ride a bicycle. He could still play certain pieces of music. The hippocampus was gone. The capacity to learn was not.

Some part of him was still receiving. Some other door was still open.

This too is what Lashley found. The brain is not a storehouse from which memory must be retrieved. The brain is a structure of doorways — and removing one doorway closes one kind of access while leaving others perfectly intact. The man who could not remember his doctors could still ride a bicycle, because the bicycle was not stored in the hippocampus. The bicycle was held somewhere else, and another door reached it.

The iceberg of mind has not been cracked because the cracking has been done from the wrong angle. The mind is not a thing inside the head whose interior must be exposed. The mind is a relationship between the head and the field. The relationship has been studied extensively from one side. The other side has barely been mapped.

• • •

The Traditional Mindology

The contemplative traditions of every civilisation developed elaborate descriptions of the mind that match, with surprising precision, the field-access model. They did not have the language of fields and access. They had the language of layers, of channels, of presences, of chambers.

The Hindu tradition speaks of multiple *koshas* — sheaths of being that envelop the soul, each operating at a different layer. The physical body is the outermost. The mind is one of the inner sheaths. Beyond the mind are the layers of intellect, of bliss, of the self that contains all the others. Memory, in this account, is held at a layer beyond the physical body, and the body accesses what is held there.

The Christian tradition, particularly in its contemplative streams, speaks of the soul as something distinct from but operating through the body. The soul carries the person across the threshold of death because the soul is not located in the body. The body is the soul's vehicle in this life. The memory is the soul's, not the body's. The body accesses what the soul contains.

The Buddhist tradition speaks of the *storehouse consciousness* — the *ālaya-vijñāna* — which holds the seeds of all experiences across all lifetimes. The brain accesses what the storehouse holds. The storehouse is not in the brain. The brain accesses the storehouse through its own doorway.

These descriptions, developed independently across cultures, converge on the same model. Memory is held somewhere other than the body. The body accesses what is held. The accessing is real. The location is not in the body. This is what Lashley found. This is what neuroscience has continued to find. The traditions had it correctly thousands of years ago. The science has been catching up, slowly, and has not yet admitted the catching up to itself.

• • •

But First, Some Homework

Before the rest of the book proceeds, the reader is asked to do a small piece of work.

Sit somewhere quiet, with no phone, no book, no music, for at least ten minutes. Close your eyes. Do not try to do anything. Just notice what arrives in your mind.

Memories will arrive. Some will be recent. Some will be from years ago. Some will be from your childhood. Notice that you did not summon them. They arrived. *The arrival itself is the data.*

At times, you may notice responses within the body — subtle shifts, sensations, or changes in feeling. These, too, are part of what is to be observed as you read. The how, the why, and what may be done will follow.

Notice also that some memories arrive with strong feeling and others arrive without. Notice that the same memory, returned to on different days, can arrive with different feelings on different days. Notice that some memories you can hold easily, while others slip away as soon as you try to hold them. Notice that some memories seem to come from outside, while others seem to rise from inside, even though the difference between outside and inside is not easy to articulate.

In quiet attention, you may also notice responses within the mind and the body — feelings, shifts, and movements that accompany what arrives. Some memories seem to draw you toward them, while others pass without hold. At times, simply noticing them — without pursuit — brings a subtle easing.

This homework is the first practice of the discerning life.

The book asks the second.

• • •

The brain is not where memory lives.

The brain is the door through which memory enters.

The door is real. The room is on the other side.

This book is about learning to see and to understand what is in the room.

CHAPTER THREE

Let us Do Some Chemistry of Spirits

"God is a mathematician," wrote Sir James Jeans.

"My God is a chemist — where physics is applied with mathematical precision."

Behind every chemical the body produces, a chemist is at work — working with elements science has not yet learned to name.

• • •

The Opening Innovation — God Is a Chemist

Sir James Jeans, one of the great physicists of the twentieth century, looked at the mathematics underlying the universe and concluded with a sentence that has endured for nearly a century: *God is a mathematician.*

He meant that the universe is structured on precise mathematical principles — so elegant they do not appear accidental. Behind creation is a mind that thinks in numbers.

This work approaches the same universe through a different lens: the atomic assembly of body and spirit. The precise combinations that give rise to life, consciousness, craving, torment, relief, and clarity.

One element combined in one way produces water. In another, fire. In another, the air we breathe.

What if similar precision operates beyond what is currently measured?

This is not a refutation of Jeans. It is an extension.

Jeans saw the calculation. Here, the attention turns to the laboratory in which that calculation is applied.

Behind creation may not be only a mind that counts. It may be also a process that combines — one that assembles, arranges, and determines which combinations sustain and which disturb.

What may be called *a periodic table of the unseen*, it is suggested, could be as precise, as lawful, and as open to inquiry as the periodic table of the physical world.

• • •

The Hierarchy

The hierarchy reads as follows:

Chemistry → *Physics* → *Mathematics* → *Biology* → *Life*

Mathematics governs how the laws of physics operate with precision. Physics governs how chemicals combine. Chemistry assembles itself, under physical and mathematical constraint, into biology. Biology, in its highest form, becomes life — the conscious, breathing, perceiving creature that the entire chain has been constructing.

And at every level, the precision is so exact, so consistent, so unrepeatable by accident, that it points toward a mind behind the calculation. Every leaf, every cell, every snowflake, every human fingerprint is a unique mathematical solution expressed chemically through physical laws. No two are identical. All are precise.

This is what Beaugrun means by chemistry as the level at which we can see the work most clearly. The mathematics is invisible. The physics is invisible. But the chemistry is *visible* — it produces the substances we can hold, the bodies we inhabit, the world we walk through. The chemistry is where the calculation becomes the world.

• • •

The Body as Chemistry

Modern science says the human body operates through chemical signals from neurons. Chemicals released at the gaps between cells. Hormones flowing through the blood. Neurotransmitters carrying messages from one part of the body to another. This is not disputed. The body is a vast laboratory of ongoing chemistry, and almost every visible action of the body — heartbeat, breath, thought, movement, mood — is mediated by chemical exchange.

Fair enough.

But the honest question, the one science does not ask, is: *what triggers the neuron to produce the chemical in the first place?*

The neuron does not self-ignite. Something initiates it. Something precedes the chemical. And if we follow that chain backward — past the neuron, past the synapse, past every measurable biological event — we arrive at a force that has no chemical explanation.

Beaugrun proposes that this force is the spirit. And if the spirit initiates the chemical, then the spirit is the chemist. The body is the laboratory. The neuron is the instrument. What we call brain chemistry may be, in honest terms, *spirit activity translated into biological language.*

• • •

The Reverse Proposition

If spirits trigger chemicals in humans, then spirits themselves may operate according to something analogous to chemistry. Not identical. But structurally similar.

Combinations. Reactions. Compounds. Valences of spiritual force.

Some spirits combining with others produce specific effects, just as hydrogen and oxygen produce water. The classical descriptions of *hell fire* and *hell darkness*, in this reading, may not be metaphors at all. They may be descriptions of specific spirit chemistries. Different combinations producing different torments. Different compounds producing different liberations.

This is the storyteller's wondering, not the scientist's certainty. The reader is invited to consider whether the observations carry weight. They are not asked to believe.

• • •

The Scriptural Anchors — Hell Fire, Hell Darkness

The Book of Wisdom, in chapter two, verse three, says: *"Our spirit shall pass away as soft air, and our life shall pass away as the trace of a cloud."* The dissipation of spirits. They do not simply vanish. They disperse — like a gas, like a compound breaking apart. This is chemistry language in ancient scripture, written long before the periodic table existed.

In Peter's letters, *hell fire* is named — not merely punishment as location, but fire as a *spirit state.* A specific combination of spiritual forces producing consuming, unquenchable effect. The image is chemical in its precision, even if the language is theological in its register.

And in First Corinthians fifteen, verse forty-four, Paul makes a structural distinction that has been read for two thousand years and rarely read carefully: *"It is sown a natural body. It is raised a spiritual body. There is a natural body and there is a spiritual body."* Paul may be read not only as speaking poetically, but as drawing a structural distinction. Two bodies. Same person. Different assembly. Different atomic configuration. Different chemical composition operating at a different frequency of matter.

The resurrection body, in Paul's careful description, is not a ghost. It is not formless light. It is a *body* — Paul insists on the word — assembled from the same raw material but configured differently. Spiritually configured. Chemically spiritual.

• • •

The Atomic Foundation

Every living being, when reduced to its most fundamental level, is atomic. Not metaphorically. Literally. Carbon, hydrogen, oxygen, nitrogen — assembled in precise combinations to produce skin, bone, neuron, blood. The body is chemistry. This is not disputed. Science and scripture agree here.

But then the leap arrives, and it is a genuine leap that the chapter offers as its central proposition.

If the physical body is atomic assembly — and First Corinthians fifteen tells us there is a spiritual body distinct from the physical body — then the spiritual body is also an assembly. A different assembly. A finer assembly. But an assembly, nonetheless.

Not nothing. Not formless void. Structured. Composed. Chemical in its own dimension.

Here a small and largely forgotten chapter in the history of medical science is worth a brief telling, because the question it dared to ask has never quite been put to rest.

In 1901, in a small sanatorium in Haverhill, Massachusetts, the physician Duncan MacDougall set up a delicate scale and began — with the consent of his terminal patients — to weigh them in the moments of their dying. He measured six in all, mostly tuberculosis patients whose moment of death could be predicted with reasonable precision. He recorded the weight of each at the instant the breath left the body, and then again a moment later, watching the needle on his scale.

The first patient, MacDougall reported, lost three-quarters of an ounce — about twenty-one grams — in that single instant. The other patients showed varying losses. He published his results in *American Medicine* in

1907, proposing, with the cautious language of a man who knew he would be mocked, that what he had measured might be the weight of the departing soul.

The medical establishment dismissed his methods, his sample size, his instruments, his conclusions. They were probably right to do so. The science was thin. The number twenty-one grams entered popular legend and was eventually borrowed for the title of a film.

And yet — the question MacDougall had been bold enough to ask was not thin at all. *If something leaves the body at the moment of death — and the religious traditions of every age insist that something does — must it be entirely without weight?* The instruments of 1907 could not honestly answer this. The instruments of the present age, perhaps, are still searching for the right calibration.

• • •

The Dark Matter Wondering

Here the chapter touches the frontier of modern physics, and what it touches must be handled carefully because the science itself is open.

Modern cosmology has identified that approximately twenty-seven percent of the universe is what scientists call *dark matter* — invisible, undetectable by current instruments, yet gravitationally real. It holds galaxies together. It bends light. It has mass and presence, without being observable by any tool science currently possesses. What dark matter actually is, remains one of the great open questions of contemporary physics.

The story of dark matter is itself worth pausing on, because it shows what happens when the world quietly proves to be larger than we had thought.

In 1933, the Swiss astronomer Fritz Zwicky was studying the Coma Cluster — a vast collection of over a thousand galaxies bound together by gravity. He measured how fast the galaxies were moving, then calculated, by Newton's perfectly reliable laws, the amount of mass that must be present to hold them together. The number he arrived at was *four hundred times* the mass of all the visible matter in the cluster.

There was, in other words, an enormous quantity of *something* in the cluster that he could not see, could not photograph, could not measure with any instrument then available. He gave it a name in German — *dunkle Materie*, dark matter — and the world's astronomers, almost without exception, ignored him for the next forty years.

It took until the 1970s, when the American astronomer Vera Rubin patiently measured the rotation of dozens of galaxies and found the same anomaly in every one of them, for the field finally to admit what Zwicky had been saying since 1933. The universe, it turned out, was filled with something that did not show itself to any tool we had yet built. *Most of what existed was not, by our usual measure, there.*

The *Beaugrun proposition*, offered as wondering rather than as claim, is this. Dark matter may not be emptiness. It may be densely populated with minute atomic particles — the atomic residue and substance of spirits. The spirit realm may not be a separate supernatural dimension floating above the physical. It may be the physical, at a level of density and fineness that current instruments cannot yet measure.

When a human being dies — which happens when the chemical form of energy comes out of the body — the physical assembly dissipates. The atomic particles that constructed the body do not vanish. They remain in this universe. *Where do they go?* This is where various cross-disciplinary perspectives meet at the same wondering. Particles do not disappear. They redistribute. They recombine. They participate in something larger than the single life they had been holding together.

The chapter does not claim that this is what dark matter is. The chapter claims only that the question is open, that the older traditions have been describing something that the newer physics has not yet ruled out, and that the convergence between them deserves the reader's attention.

This remains a possibility, not an established conclusion.

• • •

Death and Recombination

Now the hierarchy extends, in the storyteller's wondering, to its full arc. The hierarchy may be read as follows:

Chemistry → Physics → Mathematics → Biology → Life → Death → Dissipation → Recombination → New Life

If the atomic particles of every dissipating body re-enter the cosmic field, where do they go? The universe is expanding rapidly, faster than any earlier cosmology had supposed.

Could the rapid expansion of the universe carry within it the seeds of lives once lived here? Could there be, in another region of the expanding cosmos, particles that once held together what we knew as a person, now held together as something else?

This is not doctrine. This is the edge of honest wondering. The reader is invited to walk to the edge and look. They are not asked to plant a flag.

And here, before leaving the edge, one further fact deserves to be held — because it has the unusual quality of being both spectacular and proven.

Every atom of carbon in your body — every atom of nitrogen, of oxygen, of iron in your blood, of calcium in your bones, of zinc in your nerves — was forged in the heart of a star. The hydrogen alone is original, born of the universe's first moments. Everything else was cooked up in the nuclear furnaces of stars that lived and died long before our solar system existed. When those stars exhausted their fuel and exploded as supernovae, they scattered their elements into space, and from that scattering, eventually, came our planet. From our planet, eventually, came us.

The American astronomer Carl Sagan put this in a single sentence that has been quoted ever since: *"We are made of star-stuff."* He meant it literally, not metaphorically. Every breath you take draws into you atoms that have been parts of stars, oceans, dinosaurs, forests, kings and beggars across the long history of the earth.

The atomic recycling that this chapter has been describing as a *wondering* is, at the level of physical matter, the established scientific record. We do not need to speculate about whether atoms of dissipating bodies re-enter the cosmic field. They demonstrably do.

The only honest question that remains is how much *more* — beyond the atoms we have learned to measure — also re-enters the field.

• • •

The Beaugrun Position

To gather what the chapter has proposed, with the framing held clearly so the reader understands what they are being offered.

The body is chemistry. The chemistry is governed by physics. The physics is governed by mathematics. Each level is precise. Each level points to a mind behind the calculation.

The trigger that produces chemistry in the body comes from beyond chemistry. Beaugrun proposes the trigger is the spirit. The spirit is the chemist. The body is the laboratory.

If spirits initiate chemistry, spirits themselves may operate according to combinations and reactions that are structurally analogous to chemistry. Different spiritual combinations producing different effects in the persons they operate through.

The physical body and the spiritual body, as Paul distinguished them, may be two assemblies of the same fundamental substance, configured at different frequencies of matter. The dispersal of the body at death may not be its end but its dissipation into the field from which new combinations may form.

• • •

Closing

As there is no limitation for thinking, these proposals can be stated as presumptions, not claimed as doctrine. The storyteller has spoken what the storyteller has observed and wondered. The reader has been invited to consider, not commanded to accept.

Good storytelling has carried truth further than doctrine alone ever could. The reader who walks away from this chapter holding the question — *what if the chemistry of the body is the visible report of a chemistry of spirit operating beneath it?* — has been given a question worth carrying.

• • •

Thinking is not merely the interaction of neurochemicals.

Every word that comes to you has a motive.

Never ignore inner words.

CHAPTER FOUR

A Walkover from Mindnullness to Mindfulness, and How to Maintain the Pace

There is a state called mindnullness that operates beneath conscious awareness — attention is present but not inhabited.

The walkover is the practice by which this state is exchanged for mindfulness.

The pace is what allows the exchange to remain.

• • •

The Word Itself

The word *mindfulness* has, over the past decades, drifted from its original meaning by the wellness industry. It has come to mean, in popular usage, a kind of relaxed attention to the present moment — a calming practice that produces stress reduction, better sleep, improved focus.

These benefits are real, and the practices that produce them are not dismissed here.

But the original word, in the contemplative traditions that gave it to us, meant something sharper. *Mindfulness was the cultivated capacity to notice what was operating in oneself, with sufficient precision that the act of noticing begins to alter what is operating.* It was not relaxation. It was discernment, applied with care, to the inner life.

It was the American philosopher and physician William James, founder of modern psychology, who first gave the wandering mind a name in the West. In his *Principles of Psychology*, published in 1890, he described what he called the *stream of consciousness* — the continuous, unbidden flow of thoughts, images, fragments of speech, and half-remembered scenes that runs through the mind whether the thinker attends to it or not. James was not celebrating this stream. He was diagnosing it. *"The faculty of voluntarily bringing back a wandering attention,"* he wrote, *"over and over again, is the very root of judgement, character, and will."* The capacity to notice the wandering, and to gently bring attention back, was for James the foundation of every other faculty a mature human possesses. The wellness industry, much later, would borrow the practice but quietly abandon the seriousness with which James had named it.

This chapter uses the older, sharper meaning. The reader who comes to the chapter expecting the wellness version will be reoriented gently. The reader who comes expecting the contemplative version is in the right place.

And the chapter introduces a counterpart term, offered here as a diagnostic complement to mindfulness.

Mindnullness.

This word does not appear in the older traditions. It is offered here, under the small banner of the school of thought from which this book is written, as a name for a condition the older traditions described in many languages but never quite gathered under a single English term. *Where the inherited words still fit, they will be used as found. Where they bend, a new term will be coined, the elder house credited, and the difference stated in plain English.* This is the first such coinage the reader will meet.

Mindnullness is the state in which attention has been emptied without awareness. The mind has been quietly nulled. Thoughts pass without leaving a trace in conscious memory. Time passes, yet the practitioner cannot account for what was attended to within it.

This is not mindfulness, which produces full awareness. It is not sleep, which produces a clear absence. *Mindnullness is being awake without being present* — having attention without it landing on anything that can later be recalled.

Most modern adults spend a significant portion of their lives in mindnullness without recognising it as a distinct state. This chapter examines the walkover from this condition to its alternative.

• • •

How Do We Move from Mindnullness to Mindfulness?

The walkover is not a single act. It is a sustained practice. But it can be described in a way that offers a clear starting point.

It begins with *noticing the difference.* Most people have never been told that mindnullness is a separable condition. They experience it. They live through it. But without a name, there is no way to recognise when it is present. *Naming, by itself, begins the shift.* Once the concept is acquired, it becomes possible to notice when it is operating.

The practice continues with *periodic checking.* Several times during the day, one pauses briefly and asks: *What have I been doing for the last hour? What was I attending to? What thoughts were present?*

If the answer is clear and detailed, mindfulness was operating. If it is vague, or cannot be recalled, mindnullness was present — and has now been noticed.

That noticing is the practice. What is seen begins to loosen. When this is done repeatedly, day after day, the act of noticing becomes more natural, and mindnullness begins to operate with less continuity. It does not disappear. It becomes thinner — interrupted more often by awareness.

Sustained over time, this produces a change in inner condition. A larger portion of the day is spent in mindfulness, and a smaller portion in mindnullness. The proportions shift. *The shift is the practice.*

Over time, the practice becomes a way of living — the beginning of the discerning life.

• • •

The Effects Are Not the Cause

Wellness literature, in its enthusiasm for mindfulness, has introduced a confusion that must be addressed. It describes the *effects* of mindfulness — calm, clarity, focus, equanimity — and often treats these effects as the *goal* of the practice. The reader is encouraged to pursue these states, with the assumption that mindfulness will produce them.

This confuses cause and effect.

Mindfulness, in its older sense, is not a method for producing calm. *It is a capacity for noticing what is operating.* That noticing may produce a degree of calm, because what was previously unnoticed begins to lose its hold. But calm is not the aim. Noticing is.

The reader who pursues calm may be disappointed when it does not arrive on demand. The reader who pursues noticing receives whatever calm emerges — without depending on it.

This distinction matters. The walkover from mindnullness to mindfulness is not a project to feel better. *It is a movement toward clearer seeing.* Feeling may follow. But it is not what the seeing is for.

• • •

Places, Buildings, Premises

The walkover is also place-dependent in ways the reader must learn to recognise.

Some places make mindfulness easy. A forest at dawn. An empty church before the service. A library in the early morning. A kitchen after everyone has gone to sleep. In such places, the shift happens almost without effort. Mindnullness recedes. Mindfulness arrives. Attention settles without being forced.

Other places make mindfulness difficult. A crowded mall. A busy office. A room where a difficult conversation is about to begin. The home of someone whose presence, for reasons not easily explained, feels depleting. In such places, mindfulness must be cultivated against resistance. To remain attentive here requires a different kind of effort.

The chapter on disturbed places, later in the book, will explore this more fully. For now, simply notice the pattern. *Where is mindfulness easy for you? Where is it difficult?*

Over time, the map you form will begin to reveal the field through which you have been moving.

• • •

The Diagnostic by Contrast

One of the most useful ways to recognise whether mindfulness or mindnullness is operating is through *contrast between two consecutive moments.*

Notice how you feel right now, having read these last several paragraphs. Then recall how you felt thirty minutes ago, before you began. The contrast — if there is one — is the diagnostic. Something has shifted. Either the movement is toward mindfulness, in which case you are more present now than you were before, or toward mindnullness, in which case you are less present, despite having been reading and attending.

This contrast can be harsh in one direction. To realise that twenty minutes have passed without being able to recall what was read is to catch mindnullness in operation. The recognition may bring a moment of discomfort. *That discomfort is not the problem. The recognition is the practice.* What has been seen begins to loosen.

In the other direction, the contrast is kinder. To notice that time has passed and that you feel more present, more attentive, more inhabited than before, is to see the walkover at work. The reading itself became the practice. The increase in presence is the report that the practice is taking hold.

That this condition is widespread, and not the failing of a few inattentive readers, has been measured. In 2010, two researchers at Harvard — Matthew Killingsworth and Daniel Gilbert — published a study in the journal *Science* using a smartphone application that contacted thousands of participants at random moments throughout their day. The application asked three questions: *What are you doing? Are you thinking about something other than what you are doing? How do you feel?*

The result was striking. Across nearly a quarter of a million data points from over two thousand adults, participants reported their minds were *not on what they were doing* roughly forty-seven percent of the time. Almost half of waking life. And — here was the harder finding — participants were measurably less happy in the moments when their minds had wandered, regardless of what they had wandered toward. The pleasant fantasies made them no happier than the unpleasant worries did.

The researchers titled their paper, with quiet honesty, *A Wandering Mind Is an Unhappy Mind.* The chapter you are reading is naming, in a different vocabulary, what their data measured.

• • •

The Wandering and the Trap

The mind, untrained, wanders. This is well known. It is the standard subject of mindfulness instruction in contemporary wellness literature.

What is less often recognised is that *the wandering is not random.* It follows tracks. The mind returns to the same places repeatedly — the same memory, the same anxiety, the same fantasy, the same grievance, the same craving. The wandering is rutted, shaped by years of repetition.

The difficulty arises when *awareness of this wandering is mistaken for its resolution.* One notices a familiar thought, acknowledges it, and returns attention to the breath or the body. A few minutes later, the same pattern returns. The cycle continues.

In this way, noticing can become a form of accommodation rather than change. The rut remains undisturbed. Attention briefly shifts, then falls back into the same track. The walkover does not occur. Mindnullness continues in a subtler form.

Moving beyond this requires more than noticing. At the moment of recognition, a question must be allowed: *why does this pattern return? What is the wandering serving?*

Turning toward the source begins to weaken the pattern. What is examined begins to loosen. Over time, the repetition loses its hold, and the walkover begins to take place.

• • •

The Disguise of Autonomy

Mindnullness often presents itself as autonomy. One assumes they are choosing what they are doing — that attention is their own, that thoughts belong to them, that actions arise from deliberate decision.

The disguise is convincing because it operates from within. It cannot easily be seen while one is in it. *The very sense of autonomy becomes the evidence taken for awareness.*

This helps explain its persistence. Many common approaches to change — setting goals, making decisions, applying willpower — operate within the condition already shaped by it. Goals are set within it. Decisions arise within it. Effort is applied within it. The condition remains, even as surface arrangements shift.

The walkover begins when the disguise is questioned. *What appears as autonomy may not be complete.* Thoughts may not be entirely self-generated. Decisions may be influenced by what operates beneath awareness.

To recognise this is not to deny autonomy, but to see its limits. That recognition can be humbling. And in that humbling, a different kind of autonomy begins to emerge — one that is less assumed, and more consciously held.

• • •

The Seduction Sequence

There is a recurring pattern by which mindnullness reasserts itself in those who have begun the walkover. It is worth naming, because it appears in nearly every case.

It begins with success. The practice has been steady. Mindnullness has been noticed and interrupted. A sense of progress becomes visible.

Then comes a small relaxation. After some success, the practice loosens slightly. A morning check is skipped. An evening review is set aside. *Just this once.* Nothing seems to be lost.

Gradually, the relaxation becomes absorbed into the new normal. What was occasional becomes routine. The practice is quietly diminished, often without being noticed.

Weeks or months later, the condition returns. Mindnullness reasserts itself. The earlier clarity fades. What had been working appears undone.

The way through is to recognise the pattern early. *The small relaxation is not insignificant. It is the point on which the entire sequence turns.*

To see it at that moment is to interrupt the sequence. The practice holds. The walkover continues.

• • •

The Visible Sign

There is often a visible sign in those in whom mindnullness is operating — something a careful observer may begin to notice.

It appears in the eyes. There can be a quality of slight absence — an unfocused or clouded look, even when the person is awake and outwardly engaged. The shift is subtle. It is sometimes most noticeable in unguarded moments, such as photographs taken when the subject is unaware. *What is seen may not align with what is being expressed.*

After a sustained walkover, this quality can change. The eyes appear more present. They meet other eyes more directly. What contemplative traditions have called *clarity* becomes visible — not as something mystical, but as a simple report of attention being fully inhabited.

With time, this becomes easier to notice. Some encounters feel marked by presence, others by absence. The difference is not aesthetic. It reflects, in a quiet way, how attention is being held.

• • •

When the Spirit Steps Out

There is one further phenomenon worth naming, because those who continue the walkover may encounter it. Naming it in advance helps prevent confusion when it arises.

At times, in the midst of practice, there can be a moment in which something seems to lift or fall away. The phrasing is imperfect, but the experience is distinct. What had been operating within no longer feels present. The surrounding space appears altered. Thoughts that had been persistent seem to recede. The body may feel lighter.

In such moments, it can feel as though *something has stepped out* — though whether this is experienced as internal or external is not always easy to determine.

Reports of similar experiences appear across contemplative traditions. The language differs — *release, clearing, lifting* — but the pattern is familiar. Something that had been active is no longer active.

When such a moment occurs, nothing particular is required. It may simply be noticed, acknowledged, and allowed. The conditions that made it possible — sustained attention, careful noticing, and reduced drift into mindnullness — are the same conditions that support further change.

Sustained over time, these conditions can produce a gradual clearing. Not sudden, not final — but cumulative.

• • •

Maintaining the Pace

The chapter closes with the question that eventually arises: *how is the pace maintained?*

The walkover is not a destination. It is a continuous practice. There is no final point of arrival — only the ongoing cultivation of mindfulness alongside the recurring pull toward mindnullness. The pace, once established, is sustained through attention.

It is maintained by the same practices that produced it. Periodic checking. Catching the wandering at its source. Recognising the pattern of drift. Continuing through discouragement. Returning, after each lapse, to what was interrupted.

Over time, something begins to change. What once required effort becomes more natural. Awareness settles more easily. Mindnullness still appears, but it is noticed sooner, and the return is quicker. The result is not perfection, but a different baseline — more stable, more inhabited.

There is also a quieter effect. Presence begins to register beyond the individual. In some encounters, one person's clarity seems to invite another into greater attention. Without instruction, without effort, something shifts.

The walkover, sustained, has this quality. It does not remain contained. *It begins to extend.*

• • •

Closing

The walkover from mindnullness to mindfulness is the foundation of what follows in this book. The chapters ahead offer instruments — diagnostics, practices, and frameworks — but their value depends on whether the walkover has begun.

You may begin simply. Before sleep, notice what you attended to during the day. If the noticing is clear and detailed, the walkover is already underway. If it is vague, then it begins there — with the noticing of that vagueness. In either case, *the practice has started.*

• • •

Mindnullness is the disguise. Mindfulness is the unveiling.

The walkover is the movement from one to the other.

The pace is sustained by the practice that established it.

In the end, it is often visible.

PART II

Diagnostics of Disturbance

Working Instruments of Self-Observation

5. Curtail Feelings Before Emotions Conquer Behaviour

6. The Body Speaks Before the Mind Names

7. Memory Loss and Forgetfulness — A Chemical Analysis

8. Hurt Not Others — It Returns: The Boomerang Effect

CHAPTER FIVE

Curtail Feelings Before Emotions Conquer Behaviour

By the time emotion has reached the stage of producing behaviour, the person's freedom of response is significantly reduced.

The chain begins at the level of thought, where intervention is small but decisive. This chapter examines how.

• • •

There is a sequence within every human being that runs many times in a single day, often unnoticed.

A thought arrives. Something responds within. The body produces a sign — a sigh, a tightening in the chest, a quickening of the breath, a subtle pull. What is inside begins to move outward and becomes expression — a smile, a sharpened voice, a withdrawal, tears. The expression leads to action — a word spoken, a door closed, a message sent, a decision made.

By the time the action occurs, the initiating thought is often no longer remembered. The action is what the world sees. The chain that produced it remains largely invisible — except to one who has learned to observe it.

This sequence has been recognised in multiple traditions. In cognitive-behavioural frameworks, it is described as the movement from automatic thought to behavioural activation. In contemplative traditions, such as those of the desert fathers, it is described as the progression from suggestion to engagement to consent.

These traditions arose independently, separated by centuries, cultures, and methods. Yet they arrived at a similar observation. *Such convergence suggests careful attention to the same underlying reality.*

The chapter addresses how this sequence can be engaged early, before it reaches its more forceful expression.

The title points to the endpoint: emotions shaping behaviour. The word *conquer* is used deliberately. By the time emotion strongly drives behaviour, freedom of response is narrowed. Action may feel less chosen and more compelled.

This is where curtailment becomes essential. *Not suppression. Not denial.* Curtailment means attending to the sequence early enough that attention can interrupt its momentum.

The feeling is not rejected. It is noticed and named. When met at this stage, it does not gather the force that would otherwise carry it forward.

Feeling is information. Suppressing it removes that information. Curtailing it allows the message to be received without allowing the sequence to complete.

• • •

The Vessel and the Wet Patch

Imagine a vessel resting on a shelf, undisturbed. No one has poured water into it. No one has touched it. By every visible account, it should remain exactly as it was.

And yet, a wet patch appears around it.

What does the wet patch mean?

The competent response is not to wipe it away. That addresses only what is visible, not what produced it. The vessel will continue to leak onto the shelf, no matter who filled it or how often it is cleaned, because the cause lies elsewhere. Somewhere along its surface, a seam has been breached. *The wet patch is the report.*

The task is to find the leak.

This image serves as the chapter's guiding picture. The wet patch is not the problem. It is the evidence of something that has already occurred, out of sight.

Now consider the human equivalent. A person, moving through an ordinary day, suddenly finds themselves angry. There is no clear cause. The surroundings are calm. No one has acted in a way that justifies the intensity. Yet the anger rises, real and insistent.

Or fear appears without a visible threat. Or grief without a present loss. Or desire without an appropriate object. Or hostility toward someone with no apparent reason.

Each of these may be understood as a wet patch.

These cases are not rare. Any clinician who has practised long enough has met them in their consulting room — the calm professional who finds himself, on Tuesday afternoons in his own kitchen, gripped by a rage no event in his life has earned; the woman who walks into a particular hotel room while travelling and is overcome by grief for a person she does not know; the child who fears one bedroom in the house and not the others, with no history that explains it. Modern psychology, when honest, notes these in case files. The published literature, when read carefully, quietly omits them. They are inconvenient to a framework that assumes the self is a closed system, sealed off from anything but its own past.

Yet they persist. The wet patch keeps appearing. *And the framework that cannot account for it is, by that fact, incomplete.*

The response is not to manage the feeling alone, but to ask what it points to. *Why is this here? What may have preceded it? Where might the seam have been opened?*

Disproportion is the signal. When a feeling exceeds its visible cause, something in the sequence requires attention.

This must be held with care. Many feelings are proportionate. Sorrow in loss. Fear in danger. These are not to be dismissed. The concern here is with what appears *without proportion.*

Notice — while noticing is still possible.

• • •

The Reverse Approach

Most people, shaped by ordinary habits, work the chain in the wrong direction.

They notice behaviour after it has occurred. They regret it. They resolve to act differently next time. The resolution often lasts — until the chain runs again. By the time behaviour is unfolding, the capacity to alter it has already been reduced.

So attention moves one step earlier — to the emotion. Efforts are made to manage it: counting to ten, slowing the breath. Sometimes this helps. Often it does not, because by this stage the emotion has already engaged the body and the voice.

Then attention shifts further back — to the feeling itself. It is dismissed or pushed aside. *This is suppression*, and over time it can create strain rather than resolution.

The reverse approach reads the sequence differently. *It intervenes where the chain is weakest.*

That point is *thought.*

Thought is lighter, earlier, and more open to being noticed. Behaviour is heavier, more committed, and harder to redirect. By working at the level of thought, the effort is smaller and the effect more immediate.

Listening to thoughts becomes the first precaution.

With practice, a simple question begins to arise: *What is this thought? Where does it seem to be leading? Does it align with what I would consciously choose?*

Over time, differences become more noticeable. Some thoughts feel consistent with one's values and language. Others may feel unfamiliar — carrying tones, impulses, or directions that invite closer examination.

• • •

Two Vocabularies, One Sequence

What has just been described closely aligns with what cognitive-behavioural therapy identifies. Aaron Beck, working in the 1960s, described what he called the *automatic thought* — the rapid, often unnoticed thought that arises in response to a stimulus and gives rise to an emotional reaction.

It is worth noting that Beck did not arrive at this framework from outside. As is the pattern with founders of psychological methods, he came to his theory through his own experience. He suffered, throughout his life, from severe blood-injury phobia and from intense anxiety attacks, particularly while flying or speaking in public. His method was, in its first form, the discipline he had built to observe and interrupt his own anxious thoughts before they became panic. *He treated himself first. The patients came afterward.*

This is, by now, a familiar shape. Freud and his self-analysis. Jung and his confrontation with the unconscious. James and his vastation. Adler and his childhood illness. Frankl and the camps. Linehan and her own institutionalisation. Beck and his anxiety. The founders of psychology have, almost without exception, built their frameworks out of the wounds they were attempting to dress in themselves.

And here, gently, the field reaches a question it has not been able to answer. *Where do these thoughts come from?* Beck named the automatic thought. He did not, and could not, account for its source. The cognitive framework describes the thought after it has arrived. It does not ask, with any seriousness, what arrives it.

This book attempts that further question. The branch of inquiry it represents — *Soulsology*, as the school of thought from which it is written has begun to call it — does not displace psychology. Psychology has done excellent work at the level of the thought. Soulsology asks the question one step earlier: *who or what is sending the thought to be received?* Where psychology says automatic, Soulsology asks whose automation. Where psychology says trigger, Soulsology asks whose hand on the trigger. The two are not in conflict. *They are working at different depths of the same chain.*

Centuries earlier, contemplative traditions had described a similar sequence. The desert fathers spoke of *suggestion* — the thought that arrives unbidden; *engagement* — the stage in which the mind begins to turn the thought over; and *consent* — the point at which the thought is accepted and expressed in action.

From this observation, they developed a discipline of watchfulness, often called *nepsis* — a sustained attention to the inner life that allows one to notice the suggestion, observe the engagement, and interrupt the consent.

The terminology differs across the three frameworks. What is called *automatic thought* in the cognitive vocabulary resembles *suggestion* in the contemplative one. What the cognitive framework calls *appraisal* resembles what the contemplative one calls *engagement.* What becomes *behavioural activation* resembles what the older traditions called *consent.* The structure follows a similar pattern. The difference is that the contemplative tradition was always willing to ask the further question — *who is suggesting?* — that the cognitive tradition has, so far, declined to ask.

This is the bilingual method that operates throughout this book, with a third voice now beginning to be added. One reader may approach through clinical language. Another through contemplative language. A third — the reader of this book — may approach through the language Soulsology is beginning to develop. All three point toward the same underlying movement.

• • •

The Body Reports Before the Mind Names

A growing area of neuroscience points to something long observed in contemplative traditions: the body often registers changes before the conscious mind forms a clear thought.

A tightening in the chest may precede the recognition of anxiety. Heat in the face may appear before shame is named. A drop in the gut may come before fear is identified. The shoulders rise before the mind has noticed that it is bracing.

In this sense, the body acts as an earlier reporter of what is occurring within. Attention to these signals allows access to information that arrives before the mind's narrative has fully formed.

A simple practice follows. At intervals during the day, pause briefly and ask: *what is happening in the body right now?* The chest, the breath, the stomach, the shoulders, the jaw — each may be signalling something. Feelings are information.

With repeated attention, patterns begin to emerge. Subtle shifts become easier to detect. Changes are noticed earlier, sometimes before they become thoughts or actions.

• • •

The Disguise

There is a complication worth noting, because without it the diagnostic can be misleading.

The body produces sighs as part of normal physiology. At regular intervals, a deeper breath occurs to re-expand portions of the lungs affected by shallow breathing. This happens without conscious intention.

Because such signals are common, *a subtle disguise becomes possible.*

If these signals were rare, their appearance would stand out clearly. But as part of the background, variations may pass unnoticed. A change blends into what already seems ordinary.

A similar pattern can be observed in social response. When someone sighs, familiar interpretations arise — rest, fatigue, overwork. These responses are often kind. At the same time, they can shape how the moment is understood. Attention shifts. A suggestion may begin to take form.

The task here is not to reject such responses, but to examine them. In each instance, a simple question may be useful: *what is actually being felt, and what is being assumed?*

Attention to this distinction, applied carefully, becomes part of the discernment.

• • •

The Undercurrent of Waving and Patting Seems Unhealthy

There are moments when disturbance appears in unexpected forms.

Ordinarily, compliments, encouragement, and friendly gestures are understood as positive. *Well done. You look good today. I am proud of you.* These are taught as expressions of kindness, and often they are.

Yet experience is not always so simple.

At times, a gesture carries more than its visible content. The words may be kind, yet the response they leave behind may feel mixed — subtly heavy, unsettled, or unclear. *What is received is not always identical to what is said.*

Many people recognise this pattern. After an event filled with appreciation and praise, one returns home expecting lightness yet feels something different. The interaction was genuine. The warmth was real. Yet the after-effect does not fully match the moment.

Such moments invite attention, not immediate judgement. The question is not what the other intended, but what has been experienced. *Why does this remain? What continues to move in the mind after the interaction has ended?*

If a person or moment continues to repeat inwardly — through images, phrases, or emotional residue — it may be worth examining more closely. Not to accuse, but to understand.

The work here is inward. It is not a rejection of others, nor a public response. It is a quiet clarification — recognising what is felt, allowing it to settle, and returning attention to what remains stable.

Discernment, in such moments, is not suspicion. *It is careful noticing.*

• • •

The Practices

The breath practice.

When a feeling is noticed, attention is brought to the breath. The breathing slows. The exhalation lengthens. The body's activation, which had been building, begins to settle. As the breath slows, the nervous system shifts toward a more regulated state. What was gathering force begins to ease.

The naming practice.

What is present is named in simple terms: *this is anger, this is fear, this is desire, this is grief.* The naming is not judgement. It is recognition. Research suggests that naming an emotion can reduce its intensity. It introduces a small but important separation between what is felt and the one who is noticing it.

The delay practice.

A simple commitment is made in advance: *when a strong feeling arises, there will be a pause before speaking or acting.* The commitment is formed in a calm moment, so that when intensity appears, the pause is already in place. Often, by the time the delay passes, the urgency has softened.

The body-scan practice.

Attention turns to the body. Where is the feeling located? The chest, the stomach, the throat, the jaw. Once located, the feeling is allowed to be present, without forcing it to change. Under steady attention, it often begins to shift on its own.
This is *curtailment* — the practice the chapter has been pointing toward.

• • •

Curtailment Is Not Suppression

This distinction matters. Without it, the practice can be misunderstood.

Suppression refuses the feeling. It says: this should not be here. The feeling is pushed away, avoided, or covered by distraction. It is treated as something to be removed.

Curtailment takes a different approach. The feeling is noticed and named. It is allowed to be present. Attention stays with it, without rushing to act. The escalation is interrupted, but the feeling itself is not denied.

One seeks to eliminate the feeling. The other allows it to pass without letting it take control.

The difference is subtle, but decisive.

• • •

Personality Traits and the Unseen Energy Link

A trait can be understood as the cumulative result of many sequences running over time. Each begins with a moment of contact, gives rise to a feeling, moves through the body, and reaches expression in behaviour. Repeated often enough, these patterns become consistent. Observers describe them as traits: *he is anxious, she is short-tempered.* The descriptions are accurate — but they describe the surface.

What lies beneath is the repetition of the sequence itself, carried out over years without being noticed.

And here the chapter's title points to something the cognitive frameworks have not yet named. *The unseen energy link.* If a person's anger has been a repeated, unaccounted-for visitor across a lifetime, with no event in their history that explains it, the question Soulsology is willing to ask is whether that anger is entirely *theirs.* It may be a current that has been routed through them by something they have, without knowing it, given consent to. Generations of inheritance carry such currents — the temper that runs through three sons, none of whom met the grandfather it began with. So do places. So do gatherings. So do certain relationships, in which a particular feeling rises only in the company of one particular person and recedes the moment they leave the room. The trait, in such cases, is not entirely the person's own. It is the report of an energy that has been linking them to something else.

The cognitive practice still applies. Curtailment still works. The chain is still interruptible at the level of thought. But the deeper repair, when the link is recognised, is to attend to the link itself — to ask what is being conducted through, and whether the conduction can be quietly closed. *That work belongs to the chapters ahead.*

If personality reflects the accumulation of these patterns, then attending to the sequence begins, gradually, to reshape it.

Change is not immediate. A pattern built over decades does not disappear in weeks. But with repeated attention, something begins to shift. The pattern appears less frequently. When it does appear, it is less intense. And when it is less intense, it becomes easier to interrupt.

What once seemed fixed begins to show movement.

The process is gradual, but real. And it remains available to anyone willing to attend to it.

• • •

Closing

This chapter has presented both a sequence and a practice.
The sequence traces the movement from thought to feeling, through bodily signs, into emotion, and finally into behaviour.

The practice is *curtailment* — attention applied early, before the sequence gathers force. And, gently, the chapter has introduced the question that the chapters ahead will hold open: *not only what arrives in the chain, but who or what may have sent it.* Psychology has carefully described the chain. Soulsology asks the prior question. The two together, applied in patience, are the working instruments of the discerning life.

• • •

Feeling is information. Notice what you allow to continue.

Patterns form through repetition.

What repeats shapes behaviour.

CHAPTER SIX

The Body Speaks Before the Mind Names

The body is not only the executor of action.

It is also a receiver — a quiet reporter of signals the conscious mind has not yet recognised.

Learning to read these signals is one of the earliest forms of discernment.

• • •

The Body as Antenna

Have you ever noticed a sudden shift in your body without an obvious cause?

You were fine a moment ago — alert, focused, ready. Then something changes.

A heaviness settles. The eyes slow. The jaw opens. A yawn appears.

The immediate thought is simple: *I must be tired.*

But pause. You slept well. You have eaten. The body is otherwise steady. So where did the shift come from? *Why did the body change its state without a clear request from the mind?*

The body does more than conduct decisions. It also registers changes before they are fully understood. Earlier chapters have pointed to this:

the body often reports before the mind names. A subtle expression may reveal what words conceal. A disproportionate feeling may signal something not yet visible.

This chapter gathers these observations into a more deliberate practice — learning to read the body as one channel of attention.

The body often registers shifts before the mind has formed a clear interpretation. *To notice these signals early is to have access to information that would otherwise appear only later, in thought or action.*

This claim of the chapter — that the body reports before the mind names — has been carefully measured in the laboratory.

In the 1990s, the Portuguese-American neuroscientist Antonio Damasio designed what is now called the *Iowa Gambling Task*. Volunteers were asked to draw cards from four decks. Two decks were *good* — small wins, very small losses, profitable over time. Two were *bad* — large wins, but devastating losses that produced an overall loss. The decks looked identical from the outside. The pattern had to be discovered by playing.

Damasio attached small sensors to the participants' fingertips to measure changes in skin conductance — the tiny electrical changes the skin produces under stress.

What he found has reshaped the science of decision-making. Around the *tenth card*, the participants' bodies began producing measurable stress responses whenever they reached toward the bad decks. By around the *fiftieth card*, most participants could articulate a vague "hunch" that those decks were dangerous. By the *eightieth card*, they could explain the pattern logically and in words.

The body knew at trial ten what the mind would not understand until trial eighty.

Damasio called this phenomenon the *somatic marker* — a bodily signal that registers a complex pattern long before the conscious mind has formed a thought about it. His patients with damage to the brain regions that integrate body signals — most famously a man he called Elliot — could no longer make good decisions, despite intact intelligence. They could analyse a problem brilliantly, but the body's quiet vote no longer reached them. *They had lost their first reporter.*

This is what the chapter is asking the reader to attend to. The first reporter is at work, in everyone, all the time. The question is only whether the reader has learned to read the report.

• • •

The Body That Transmits

The body, however, is not only a receiver. There is a quieter line of recent research suggesting that it is also, continuously and without our knowing, a *transmitter.*

For some years, researchers at the HeartMath Institute in California — working at the boundary where physiology meets the older traditions — have been measuring the electromagnetic field generated by the human heart. Their findings are surprising. The heart's field is approximately *five thousand times stronger* than the field generated by the brain. It is the strongest electromagnetic field the human body produces. And — this is the part the older traditions would have nodded at without surprise — it extends measurably outward from the body, several feet in all directions.

When two people sit near each other in a quiet room, their heart fields can be shown, by sensitive instruments, to influence each other. The slow, regular rhythm of one heart can entrain the other's rhythm, even when neither person is aware of the exchange. Mothers and infants do this constantly. So, the research suggests, do close friends, married couples, and people in love. So, more darkly, may persons in proximity who are quietly in conflict.

This is one piece of evidence — there are others — that the body is doing more than receiving. *It is sending.* What it sends is measurable in some respects, beyond measurement in others. The older traditions described what they called *presence* — the quality some people carry that calms or unsettles a room without a word being spoken. The instruments are now beginning to give that observation a numerical form.

For the practice this chapter describes, this carries one important consequence. The body's signals you are learning to read may not all be your own. Some of what your body is reporting may be the field of another body in the room. The chapters on disturbed places and on the boomerang effect will return to this.

For now, simply notice. The body is an antenna, yes. *It is also a small transmitter, broadcasting in a band the older traditions called spirit.*

• • •

Signals Worth Noticing

Certain body signals are worth paying attention to. They are gathered here for those developing this practice.

A yawn that arrives without clear cause.
Most yawns are biological. The body needs them. They appear with genuine tiredness. But at times, a yawn appears when these explanations do not fit — at the start of meaningful work, during prayer, or at the beginning of an important conversation. Such moments are worth noticing.

It is worth pausing on the yawn for a moment, because it is the strangest of these signals. Despite more than a century of careful research, no one has fully explained why humans yawn. The old idea that yawning brings in needed oxygen has been measured and quietly disproven. The brain-cooling theory has partial support but does not account for all cases. What recent research has begun to suggest is that yawns cluster around *transitions* — the moment of beginning a task, the moment of ending one, the moment of crossing a threshold from one state of attention to another. They appear at the boundary, not in the middle. *This is precisely the moment at which, the chapter is suggesting, the body may be reporting something other than tiredness.*

Heaviness in the eyes when alertness is expected.
The lids feel weighted. The eyes slow, even though sleep would not naturally follow.

Restlessness without occasion.
An urge to move, to check the phone, to shift position. The restlessness appears without a clear trigger.

Mood shifts without proportionate cause.
One moment there is calm. The next, irritation, sadness, or anxiety arises, greater than the situation seems to warrant. *This is the wet patch.*

Limb heaviness without exertion.
The body feels unusually heavy. Simple tasks seem harder than they should be.

Sudden forgetfulness mid-task.
An intention is present, then disappears. The thread is dropped.

Unexpected emotional expression.
Laughter in a serious moment. Tears without a clear cause. Anger that exceeds the situation.

Sudden hunger or thirst at the moment of focus.
As attention gathers, a strong urge to eat, drink, or step away arises.
None of these, taken alone, proves anything. But noticed over time, *they begin to form a pattern.*

• • •

Timing is Diagnostic

There is one observation that deserves particular attention. Signals, taken in isolation, are not always meaningful.

But notice *when* they arise.

A yawn at the moment a difficult conversation begins. Restlessness as attention deepens in prayer. Sudden hunger in the first minutes of focused work. A shift in mood at the threshold of an important decision.

Timing gives the signal its weight.

A yawn in the middle of an ordinary afternoon is usually just that — ordinary. The same signal, arriving at the exact moment something meaningful is about to begin, invites closer attention.

The task is to observe patiently over time. As patterns accumulate, their significance begins to reveal itself.

• • •

Three Layers, Not One

Body signals may arise from more than one source. They can be biological, psychological, or, as earlier chapters have suggested, interpreted within a broader framework. Often, more than one of these may be present at the same time, producing a single visible effect.

A yawn at the start of prayer may reflect simple tiredness. It may also relate to unprocessed tension about the practice. It may carry additional meaning depending on how the experience is understood. At times, several of these may overlap.

To consider only one layer is to narrow the field of understanding. *A wider attention allows patterns to be seen more clearly over time.*

• • •

Notice without Obeying

The body produces a signal. The untrained mind often responds by obeying it automatically. A yawn appears, and activity stops. Restlessness arises, and attention shifts — to the phone, to movement, to distraction.

The practice introduces a *pause* between signal and response.

The signal appears. It is noticed. What is happening in the body is named, without immediate interpretation. A breath is taken — slow, deliberate. Attention turns inward for a moment.

Then a choice is made.

Whether to continue, or to attend to what has arisen.

The decision remains one's own. *The practice lies in the noticing, not in any fixed response.*

• • •

A Caution

Most yawns are biological. Most restlessness is simply restlessness. Most hunger is just hunger.

At the beginning of this practice, there is a risk of becoming overly watchful — interpreting every bodily signal as something more than it is. *This is not the aim.* Discernment rests in proportion. When there is no clear disproportion, the signal is likely what it appears to be.

There is also a practical consideration. Persistent fatigue, low mood, difficulty concentrating, recurring intrusive emotions, or sustained anxiety that interferes with daily life deserve medical attention. The interpretive lens used in this book is *one* layer of understanding. The medical perspective is another.

Both have their place. Neither replaces the other.

• • •

Closing

The body is one of the instruments of the discerning life. This chapter has outlined the signals worth noticing, the role of timing in understanding them, the openness required to consider multiple layers, and the practice of noticing without automatic response.

And it has gently widened the picture. The body is not only an antenna receiving its own news. *It is also, quietly, a transmitter — sending into the room, into the field, into the lives of those nearby, what it is itself carrying.* What follows in the next chapter, on memory, will continue this widening.

• • •

Your body is not your enemy. It is your early reporter.

Learn its language. Read its signals.

Discern — before you obey.

CHAPTER SEVEN

Memory Loss and Forgetfulness — A Chemical Analysis

Karl Lashley searched for the physical location of memory in the brain and did not arrive at a definitive answer.
At the same time,
there are instances in which highly capable minds forget what others remember.

Forgetfulness is not always simple deletion.
It appears as disturbance, and it varies from person to person.

• • •

The Puzzle of the Eminent Forgetful

History contains many accounts of absent-mindedness among individuals whose attention, by most measures, was highly developed. Newton forgetting to eat. Einstein stepping into traffic. Thales walking into a well while observing the stars. A mathematician pouring coffee into an inkwell. A writer searching for the glasses already being worn.

These stories are often received with amused affection. Yet they point toward
a question worth examining. *How do minds capable of sustained, refined attention also display such lapses?*

Common explanations — fatigue, monotony, fluctuations in attention — account for many instances of forgetfulness. Yet they do not fully explain why such patterns appear even in those whose attention is otherwise highly developed.

What, then, is taking place?

• • •

What Science has Established

It is useful to begin with what science has mapped, because its findings are real and valuable within their scope.

Every thought, in biological terms, involves neural activity. Neurons communicate by moving ions across membranes and releasing neurotransmitters at synapses. In this sense, there is no thought without a corresponding physical process.

Thoughts, however, differ in their emotional and motivational weight. This difference is influenced by neuromodulators — such as dopamine, norepinephrine, acetylcholine, and cortisol — which help mark certain thoughts as important. *What is marked tends to be retained. What is not gradually fades.* This is one way memory becomes shaped by what attention highlights.

Within this framework, absent-mindedness can be understood as a shift in attention systems. The networks responsible for sustained, outward focus lose dominance, while internally oriented activity becomes more prominent. As this balance changes, attention to the external task weakens, and the thread is lost.

This is the standard account. The underlying chemistry is real, and much of the mechanism has been carefully studied.

• • •

Where the Standard Explanation Strains

The standard account, while useful, shows limits that careful observation can detect.

One point of tension appears in the case of highly capable yet absent-minded individuals. A deficit-based model would suggest that lapses correlate with reduced attention or low arousal. *It does not fully explain why individuals capable of sustained, refined focus also display marked moments of inattention.*

Another appears in the speed of recovery across environments. A person who feels mentally clouded in one setting may enter another — a quiet place, a natural setting, or a context of meaningful work — and find clarity returning within minutes. The shift can seem quicker than what gradual physiological recovery alone would suggest.

A third appears in pattern. For many, forgetfulness is not evenly distributed. It tends to arise at particular moments — before writing, during prayer, or in situations requiring clarity or honesty. Rather than appearing random, it can seem *patterned.*

These observations do not invalidate the standard explanation. They suggest that it may not be complete. The chemistry is real — but it may be influenced by factors not fully accounted for within chemistry alone.

There is one further case that the standard account struggles to accommodate — a case as instructive in its excess as Lashley's rats were in their loss.

In 1929, the Russian neuropsychologist Alexander Luria began to study a young Moscow journalist named Solomon Shereshevsky. The journalist had come to Luria not because he was failing at his work, but because his editor had noticed, with some unease, that he never took notes. Luria asked him to memorise a list of fifty words. The journalist did so, without effort. Then a list of seventy. Then a table of fifty numbers. Each was returned, perfectly, in any order Luria asked.

Luria continued to study Shereshevsky for the next thirty years. He could find no limit to the man's memory. Lists given to him in 1936 could be recalled, exactly, in 1959. Fifteen-year-old conversations were retrieved with the colour, scent, and posture of the room in which they had occurred. Luria eventually published a small book about him, *The Mind of a Mnemonist* (1968), which remains one of the most curious documents in twentieth-century neuroscience.

The curiosity is not what Shereshevsky could remember. It is what he *could not do*. He found ordinary conversation difficult, because every word summoned its colour, its taste, its smell, its associated memories, and the room he had first heard it in. Metaphor was nearly impossible — every phrase was literal. He could not easily recognise faces, because each glance produced a slightly different image and the small variations would not resolve. He spent years trying, with little success, to learn how to *forget*.

The case complicates the standard chemistry of memory. If forgetting were merely a deficit — a failure of the marking systems to flag what mattered — then a mind that retained everything would be a mind enriched. Shereshevsky's life suggests the opposite. *Forgetting is not the absence of memory. It is one of memory's essential operations.* What Lashley could not find in the rat's brain was, perhaps, never meant to be a permanent storage at all. It was meant to be access — selective, contextual, and gracefully incomplete.

• • •

Two Directions of Loosening

Absent-mindedness may not always arise in the same way. It can reflect different movements of attention.

One form appears as *upward absorption*. Attention becomes deeply engaged with something demanding — an idea, a problem, a line of thought. In such moments, ordinary cues are missed. Meals are forgotten. Surroundings fade. The forgetfulness reflects attention being drawn into something more absorbing than the immediate environment.

Another form appears as *disruption of ordinary focus*. Attention becomes scattered or displaced. The thread of activity is lost, not because it has been surpassed, but because it has been interrupted. What was being done slips away.

Both forms may look similar from the outside. The underlying movement differs.

To recognise the difference is useful. In one case, attention is deeply engaged. In the other, it is unsettled or fragmented. *The response in each case is therefore not the same.*

• • •

The Laughing Gas Comparison

There is a chemical example that offers a useful comparison.

Nitrous oxide — commonly called laughing gas — has been known since the early nineteenth century. The name does not imply that the gas directly produces laughter. Rather, it alters the brain's integrative systems in ways that may express as laughter in humans.

The gas affects neural activity by interacting with receptor systems and altering neurotransmitter balance. The result is a loosening of ordinary integration. Under its influence, responses that are usually moderated may become more freely expressed.

The effects are not uniform. Many experience euphoria. Others report anxiety, disorientation, or unusual perceptual states. William James, for example, described a temporary sense of profound insight while under its influence — an experience that faded when the effect passed, yet left a lasting impression about the range of human consciousness.

Animals are also affected by the gas. Their responses reflect altered neural integration, but they do not display the same outward expressions as humans. This suggests that while the chemical effect may be similar in structure, *its expression depends on the capacities of the organism.*

The comparison points to a broader consideration. Biological mechanisms are real and measurable. At the same time, their outward expression may vary depending on the system in which they operate.

The model is useful — but it has limits.

• • •

Disturbance Is Not Deletion

Absent-mindedness does not always appear as a loss of capacity. More often, it presents as a *disturbance in access*, and this disturbance may vary from person to person.

The memory may still be present. The ability to think remains. The underlying faculties are intact. What seems to change is the connection between the individual and what would otherwise be available. *Information is not necessarily lost; access to it becomes less immediate or temporarily disrupted.*

This view aligns with earlier observations. Capacity may not be removed, but obscured. What appears absent may instead be momentarily out of reach.

There is a famous illustration of this in literature, and it has its anatomy in the brain.

Marcel Proust, in the opening volume of *In Search of Lost Time* (1913), describes a moment in which the narrator, an adult who has not thought of his childhood village in decades, dips a small cake — a *madeleine* — into a cup of tea and tastes it. The taste, mingled with the scent of the lime-flower tisane, opens without warning into the entire village of his childhood: the streets, the gardens, the faces, the church spire, the long Sunday afternoons. Nothing of this had been accessible to him a moment before. *The information had not been lost. It had simply been waiting for the right key.*

There is a reason the key was a smell. Of all the senses, only olfaction bypasses the thalamus — the brain's general switching station — and travels directly into the limbic system, the older brain regions where memory and emotion are tightly woven together. A smell does not arrive as data to be processed. It arrives, more or less, as memory itself, already coloured by feeling. This is why the scent of a particular kitchen, a particular soap, a particular school corridor can collapse forty years in an instant.

The Proustian moment is not poetic exaggeration. It is a faithful report of the only sensory pathway in the human body that leads, almost without translation, into the place where memory and feeling are kept. The chapter's claim — that what appears absent may simply be momentarily out of reach — has, in this one corner of the brain, a particularly clear demonstration.

The pattern is not always uniform. Some notice lapses when attempting focused work. Others during reflective or personal moments. Rather than appearing random, such patterns can seem specific to the individual.

To observe these patterns is not to conclude too quickly, but to recognise that *forgetfulness may reflect more than simple loss.*

• • •

The Place-Dependence Diagnostic

One of the clearer observations in this chapter concerns place.

When patterns of forgetfulness appear in certain environments and ease in others, the contrast itself becomes informative. The experience in one place is real. The change in another is equally real. Placed side by side, they invite closer attention.

If such changes were entirely internal, they might be expected to shift more gradually. Yet many report noticeable differences within a short time of entering a different setting. This suggests that *context may play a more immediate role than is always assumed.*

The chapter's observation has, in fact, been measured in the laboratory — and the measurement is one of the more entertaining experiments in the literature.

In 1975, two British psychologists, Duncan Godden and Alan Baddeley, persuaded eighteen members of a Scottish diving club to participate in a memorisation experiment. The participants were asked to learn lists of forty words. Half the lists were learned on dry land. The other half were learned twenty feet beneath the surface of the sea, the divers floating in cold water with their breathing regulators hissing.

The participants were then tested for recall — some on land, some underwater. The result was striking. Words learned on land were recalled best on land. Words learned underwater were recalled best underwater. The mismatch — learning in one context, testing in another — produced roughly *forty percent fewer* remembered words.

The phenomenon has since been called *context-dependent memory*. The same word, the same brain, the same person — yet the place itself proved to be part of the memory. Without the surrounding cold water, the diver's memory had less to hold onto. The surrounding context, it appeared, was not a neutral container for what the mind held. *It was part of how the mind held it.*

This is precisely what the chapter has been observing about clouded thought returning when one enters a different room. The science has, since 1975, been pointing in the same direction. *Place is not the backdrop of memory. It is one of its hooks.*

The observation does not replace existing explanations. It adds another layer to them. Environment, attention, and internal state may be interacting in ways not fully captured by a single model.

The contrast, observed over time, becomes the diagnostic.

• • •

The Both-And Posture

Memory and forgetfulness may arise from multiple sources. They can be biological. They can be psychological. They may also be understood within broader interpretive frameworks. Often, more than one of these operates at the same time.

A lapse at the threshold of meaningful action may reflect simple fatigue. It may relate to unprocessed anxiety about what is being approached. It may also be experienced in ways that earlier chapters have described. At times, these influences may overlap.

To consider only one layer is to narrow the field of understanding. *Holding more than one possibility in view allows patterns to be seen with greater clarity over time.*

• • •

Practical Discernment

The practice offered here is simple in description and gradual in its effect.

First, notice when forgetfulness appears. Over time, begin to observe the moments when attention loosens — not to resist it immediately, but to see when it occurs. Patterns, once noticed, become informative.

Second, ask a few guiding questions. *What was about to happen? Where was I? Who was present? What place had I just entered or left? What thought appeared just before the shift?* These questions do not yield instant answers, but over time they begin to form a map.

Third, distinguish the context of the lapse. At times, it may accompany deep engagement — attention drawn into something absorbing. At other times, it may appear alongside distraction, unease, or loss of focus. Noticing the difference helps guide the response.

Fourth, attend to all relevant layers. Rest well. Eat well. Seek medical advice if patterns interfere with daily life. Alongside this, continue the inner work of observation and attention.

The practice is steady, and *its clarity grows with time.*

• • •

Closing

Not all absent-mindedness reflects the same condition. At times, it may accompany deep engagement, where attention is drawn beyond ordinary awareness. At other times, it may appear as a disruption of focus at moments that matter.

From the outside, both can look similar. Both are often described in the same way. The difference lies in the underlying pattern, and in how it is understood.

Discernment allows these patterns to be approached differently — *without reducing them to a single explanation.*

• • •

The faculty is not broken.

Access may be disrupted.

The pattern is not always the same.

It varies from person to person.

Notice when it appears.

Ask what surrounds it.

Attend to what you find.

And remember —

what seems lost may still be present,

waiting for the path to open.

CHAPTER EIGHT

Hurt Not Others.
It Returns.
The Boomerang Effect

There is a saying passed down in many homes:
the words spoken about others have a way of returning — sometimes with greater weight than when they were first spoken.

What is often treated as simple wisdom invites closer examination.

• • •

Words Carry Force

Across generations, a similar teaching has appeared in different forms: *what is spoken does not end with the speaking. It leaves an imprint.*

In ordinary understanding, words carry meaning. They inform, persuade, describe. Yet experience suggests that they may also carry tone, intention, and effect that extend beyond their immediate use. A word spoken in anger does not end when it is heard. It can remain — in memory, in relationship, in the atmosphere of an interaction.

Many traditions have approached this idea in their own language. Some speak of *blessing* and *curse*. Others of *mantra* and *recitation*. Others of speech that *builds* or *destroys*. While the interpretations differ, there is a recurring observation: speech has consequence beyond its moment.

This chapter explores that observation — not as a fixed claim, but as something to be examined carefully.

Words do not simply vanish. They continue to have effects — within the speaker, within the listener, and within the shared space between them.

How those effects unfold is what this chapter seeks to understand.

There is a small form of this pattern that the careful observer can verify in their own life within a single week.

Take a person whom you currently hold with goodwill. Then, over the next few days, speak about them — to others, or even silently, to yourself — with steady criticism, dismissal, or contempt. Do this consistently, even if no one else hears. Do not change anything else about your behaviour toward them. Then, at the end of the week, watch what happens at your next direct encounter.

Something will have shifted, in spite of yourself. The other person, having heard nothing, will somehow have changed *in your eyes*. Their face will register differently. Their voice will register differently. Their movements will seem either more grating or more flat than before. They have not changed. *You have.* And the change has been built, quietly, by what you have been speaking about them.

If the small experiment were extended for a year, the alteration would be marked enough to be visible to a third party. Extended for ten years, the relationship would be unrecognisable.

This is one ordinary form of the larger pattern the chapter is naming. *Words shape the speaker first — and through the speaker, the conditions in which the speaker lives.*

• • •

The Returning Motion

The boomerang effect points to a pattern often noticed over time: *words spoken with the intent to harm can, in various ways, return to affect the speaker.*

The return is not always immediate, nor always obvious. It may appear in altered relationships, in reputation, or in the gradual shaping of one's environment. Yet, observed over longer periods, certain patterns become difficult to ignore.

Part of this can be understood in natural terms. Speech shapes the speaker. Words spoken repeatedly influence habits of attention, tone, and response. What is said once becomes easier to say again. Over time, a pattern forms. Others begin to respond to that pattern. Trust may weaken. Opportunities may narrow. Relationships may shift.

In this sense, what returns is not a direct reversal, but the consequence of what has been formed over time.

Some have also described an additional layer — one in which expression appears to influence the wider field of interaction. In this view, what is repeatedly expressed may be reflected back in experience, not as immediate cause and effect, but as a pattern that gathers over time.

Whether understood in purely social terms or in a broader interpretive sense, the observation remains: *what is spoken does not end with the speaking. It continues to shape both the speaker and the conditions in which they live.*

There is a particular feature of this returning motion that deserves clearer attention than common usage gives it.

The phrase *what goes around comes around*, in popular speech, is often taken to mean that harm somehow doubles back on the one who sent it — a kind of universal revenge, with the world keeping a small ledger and settling it one day. The observation behind the phrase is sound. The interpretation common to it is not.

Newton's third law of motion states that for every action there is an equal and opposite reaction. The textbook image is of two billiard balls, one striking the other, the force passing cleanly between them. The force does not return to the first ball as punishment. It does not chase it. *It distributes itself through the field in which the action occurred.*

What the author has observed, across long watching, is that the same lawful pattern operates in the field of speech and thought. A word sent out as harm does not return as a counter-blow aimed at the sender. The sender is not chased. There is no ledger. What occurs is finer, and quieter, and more difficult to escape. *The energy of the harmful word, when sent, encounters the field around it — and what it encounters does not strike back. It withdraws. It flees. It disperses.*

This pattern may be called, for shorthand, *Newton's Flight Principle.* The natural response of any spirit, any presence, any current of life that is met with harm is not to retaliate but to depart. Trust withdraws. Goodwill flees. Whatever was open, closes. Whatever was extended, returns to itself. The action did not provoke an opposite action; it provoked a *flight.*

But here is where the speaker's situation differs from the textbook billiard ball. *The speaker has not stepped outside the field.* They are still standing in it. The flight that their words produced is happening all around them. The withdrawal of trust, the closing of goodwill, the silent departure of currents that had once been turned toward them — these are now the conditions in which they live. The return is not a counter-strike. It is the new shape of the field.

This is not punishment. It is physics, observed in the realm of spirit. *The boomerang has not been thrown back at the thrower. The thrower has remained standing in the place where the throw was made and now lives in the field that the throw has emptied.*

• • •

The Other Direction

The pattern appears to move in the other direction as well. It is worth noting this with equal care, as attention is often drawn more easily to the negative side than to the positive.

Words spoken with care, respect, or encouragement also seem to carry forward. Kindness, once expressed, can shape tone, relationship, and response over time. The effects may not be immediate, but they often become visible across longer stretches.

A teacher who has spoken patiently for years may find that patience reflected in later interactions. A neighbour who consistently responds with acknowledgement and goodwill may, in times of difficulty, encounter a similar spirit in return. *These are not guarantees, but patterns that many recognise.*

The same underlying process appears to be at work. What is repeatedly expressed begins to shape both the speaker and the environment in which they move. The currents of trust and goodwill, instead of fleeing, gather more readily toward the one whose words have been steady. The field, instead of emptying, fills.

Earlier generations often expressed this simply: *speak well of others, and refrain from speaking harm.* Whether understood as moral guidance or as observation, the teaching reflects an awareness that speech has consequences beyond the moment in which it is spoken.

• • •

The Practice of the Evening

This chapter offers a simple practice that can begin at once.

Before sleep, sit quietly for a few minutes and review the day. Bring to mind the people you spoke about — whether aloud to others or inwardly in your own thoughts. For each, notice the quality of what was said or held. *Was it kind? Was it honest? Was it harmful? Was it unnecessary?*

Where speech or thought carried harm, even in small ways, take a moment to release it inwardly. The wording may be your own. A simple acknowledgement is sufficient: *that was not what I wish to carry forward. I release it. I do not hold harm toward this person.* The words matter less than the intention to let it go.

Where speech was kind, nothing further is required. Where it was honest and necessary, nothing further is required.

Over time, this practice serves two purposes. It brings awareness to the tone of one's speech and thought, and it introduces a moment of correction before the day closes. With repetition, this awareness begins to carry into the next day — *shaping what is about to be spoken before it is spoken.*

• • •

What This Practice Does

This practice does not erase what has been said. Harmful words, once spoken, remain part of what has occurred. The evening reflection does not undo them. It works in a different way.

Without reflection, patterns of speech tend to repeat. What is said once becomes easier to say again. Over time, this repetition shapes habit. Gradually, a way of speaking forms — often without being noticed.

The act of releasing interrupts this pattern. *By acknowledging and letting go of what was said, the tendency to repeat it is weakened.* The habit does not deepen in the same way.

In this sense, the practice does not remove what has been done, but it reduces the likelihood of carrying it forward unchanged.

Over time, this makes a difference. Repeated daily, the practice shapes speech in a quieter way — through awareness, restraint, and intention. *Across years, the direction it sets can become clearly visible.*

There is one further feature of the returning motion worth naming, because it explains why the return rarely arrives all at once.

When a word, an act, or a held thought is sent out, it does not produce only a single response. It enters a field full of currents, and *each current responds in its own time.* Some respond at once. Some take days. Some take years. The mind that initiated the action, however, has only a single doorway through which response can return. *It receives one at a time.*

This means that what was sent out as a single throw will, over time, return as a long line of arrivals. The first may be quick. The second may follow weeks later. The fortieth may arrive a decade after the throw, by which time the thrower has long forgotten what was thrown. The connection is not always visible to the one receiving the response. It is, however, present in the field.

The author has come to call this pattern *the Beaugrun Doorway*. It is one reason that careful speech, sustained over time, makes more difference than dramatic moments of restraint. The doorway is always open, in both directions, all day, every day. *What passes through it, in the long run, becomes the conditions of one's life.*

• • •

A Caution

This teaching requires care in its application.

It is not a call to avoid honest speech. There are times when truth must be spoken, even when it is uncomfortable. The intention is not to replace honesty with pleasantness, but to distinguish between *speech that serves* and *speech that harms.*

The honest critic, the truthful witness, the friend who speaks what is difficult to hear — these are not outside the teaching. When such speech arises from concern for the other rather than from the speaker's impulse, it carries a different quality, even if its effect is momentarily uncomfortable.

Over time, the difference becomes clearer. *Speech offered in service feels different from speech offered for satisfaction.* With practice, this distinction can be sensed before words are spoken. That sensing becomes part of the discernment.

• • •

The old teaching endures because it reflects a pattern often observed.

Words do not end with their speaking.

They continue to have effects.

Speak, then, with the awareness

that what is expressed may, in some form, return.

PART III

Discernment and Environment

Reading the World the Discerning Reader Walks Through

9. Are Natural Disasters Preplanned? Animals Discern. Why Can't Humans?

10. Spiritual and Intellectual Protection

11. Why Certain Places Disturb Us

12. Why Powerful Words Clear What Advice Cannot Move

CHAPTER NINE

Are Natural Disasters Preplanned? Animals Discern. Why Can't Humans?

Accounts from different parts of the world suggest a recurring observation: animals often behave differently before major natural events.

Whether this reflects sensitivity, instinct, or something not yet fully understood remains an open question.

• • •

The Elephants of Yala

On the morning of December 26, 2004, before the Indian Ocean tsunami reached parts of Sri Lanka, unusual behaviour was reported among animals in and around Yala National Park. Elephants moved inland. Birds abandoned low-lying areas. Some domestic animals resisted being taken outdoors. By the time the waves reached the coast, many of these animals were no longer in the most affected zones.

Large numbers of people lost their lives that day. Observers later noted that animal fatalities appeared comparatively lower, though exact figures remain difficult to establish.

Similar accounts appear across history. Before the Helike earthquake of 373 BCE, reports describe animals leaving the region days in advance. Prior to the Haicheng earthquake of 1975, unusual animal activity was among the factors that contributed to evacuation decisions. In Japan, some have noted changes in the behaviour of certain marine species before seismic events. Historical writings, including those from the time of Vesuvius, also mention animal restlessness.

The earliest detailed account of this pattern comes from the ancient world, and it deserves a closer look.

In 373 BCE, the Greek city of Helike, on the Gulf of Corinth, was struck by a powerful earthquake at night, followed by a tsunami that drowned the entire city beneath the sea. The records of what happened in the days *before* the disaster are unusually rich.

Five days before the earthquake, according to the writings of Aelian and Diodorus Siculus, the animals of Helike began to leave the city in numbers no one had seen before. Rats, snakes, weasels, centipedes, worms, beetles — all departed by visible roads, moving in steady columns toward the higher ground beyond the city walls. The people of Helike watched them go and did not understand what they were watching. By the time the ground shook, the animals were already safe and the people were not.

What is striking about the account is its specificity. The ancients did not record this as legend. They recorded it as observation — the kind of detail that does not survive without an eyewitness who stood in the road and counted what he saw. The story was old in Aelian's time, but it had been preserved with the careful precision the ancient world reserved for what it took seriously.

Helike itself was lost to the sea for over two thousand years. Recent archaeological surveys have located the ruins beneath sediment in the Gulf of Corinth. *The city is gone. The account remains.*

These accounts do not offer a single explanation. But they point to a pattern worth examining.

The question is not only whether animals respond differently, but *how*. And alongside it, another question arises: *what has changed in human attention that such signals are less often recognised?*

• • •

The Small Science of What They Detect

A natural explanation may account for much of what is observed — and in some ways, it is no less remarkable.

Elephants are known to communicate over long distances using *infrasound* — frequencies below the range of human hearing. Seismic activity often produces early waves that travel ahead of the more destructive ones, sometimes within similar low-frequency ranges. Species already attuned to such signals may be responding to changes that humans do not consciously register.

Marine species such as oarfish inhabit depths where environmental changes differ significantly from those at the surface. Some researchers have explored whether shifts in electromagnetic or geological conditions might influence their behaviour, though the mechanisms are still under study. Traditional stories, such as those linking catfish to earthquakes, reflect long-standing attempts to interpret these observations.

Birds can detect changes in air pressure before storms. Reptiles and amphibians respond to variations in ground temperature and humidity. Domestic animals may react to subtle vibrations or atmospheric changes that precede events.

These responses do not require an additional sense. *They reflect sensitivities within the known range of perception — operating at levels or in conditions humans are less attuned to.*

What appears extraordinary may, in part, be a difference in attention and sensitivity.

• • •

What We Traded Away

A more subjective question follows. *Have these sensitivities been lost — or simply diminished through changes in how we live?*

Modern life has altered our relationship with the environment. Buildings reduce exposure to weather. Vehicles limit contact with the ground. Artificial light changes our sense of natural cycles. Urban noise can mask subtler signals. These changes bring safety and convenience, but they may also reduce certain forms of awareness.

There are examples that suggest such awareness can still be present under different conditions.

Among the Moken sea nomads of the Andaman region, accounts from 2004 describe how elders recognised unusual signs — the behaviour of animals, changes in the sea, and shifts in the surrounding environment. Drawing on inherited knowledge, they moved inland before the waves arrived.

On the island of Simeulue, near the epicentre of the same event, a tradition known as *smong* had been passed down since an earlier tsunami. The teaching was simple: *when the ground shakes and the sea recedes, move to higher ground.* When the earthquake occurred, many followed this guidance, and survival rates were notably higher than in some nearby regions.

There is also a more recent example, in which the saving knowledge was acquired not through inheritance but through a single geography lesson.

In December 2004, a ten-year-old British girl named Tilly Smith was on holiday with her family at Maikhao Beach in Phuket, Thailand. Two weeks earlier, in her school in Surrey, her geography teacher had taught the class about tsunamis — how they form, what precedes them, what to watch for. The teacher had described, in particular, two signs: the strange withdrawal of the sea before the wave arrives, and the small bubbling that appears at the surface as the water shifts.

On the morning of December 26, Tilly stood on the beach and noticed the tide receding much further than seemed normal, and the surface beginning to bubble. She recognised the pattern at once. *That is what they showed us in school,* she told her parents. *We are about to see a tsunami.*

Her parents listened. They alerted the hotel. The beach was cleared. By the time the wave arrived, the stretch of sand where roughly a hundred people had been standing was empty. All of them survived.

The example is small in scale, but it points to something useful. *The forms of attention that were once carried by inheritance can also be carried, in a more compressed form, by careful teaching.* The faculty has not been lost. It only requires that someone notice it is there to be taught.

These examples point toward a possibility. *What appears as instinct may also be memory — carried, taught, and retained across generations.*

The difference may not lie in the presence or absence of ability, but in whether attention has been preserved.

• • •

Myth As Compressed Memory

Another line of observation appears in an unexpected place: traditional stories.

Among the Klamath people of Oregon, there is a long-preserved account of a great conflict that ended with the collapse of a mountain and the formation of a deep lake. Geological studies indicate that Mount Mazama did indeed erupt and collapse, forming what is now Crater Lake thousands of years ago. While the relationship between story and event is interpretive, the correspondence has drawn considerable attention.

Along the Pacific Northwest coast, oral traditions speak of a night when the ocean rose and swept inland. For many years, these accounts were treated as legend. Later research connected them with a large seismic event in 1700 along the Cascadia subduction zone, supported by records from Japan and by geological evidence along the North American coast.

Flood narratives appear across many ancient cultures. Some researchers have explored whether these accounts may reflect distant memories of large-scale environmental changes, including rising sea levels following the last ice age. The connections are not always direct, but the recurrence of such themes is notable.

These examples suggest a possibility: that stories can preserve observations across generations, especially in cultures where memory is carried through narrative rather than written record.

In this sense, *myth may function not only as symbolic expression, but also as a form of remembered experience* — shaped, compressed, and carried forward through time.

• • •

Dhanushkodi, December 1964

Along the coast of Tamil Nadu lies Dhanushkodi, once a small but active pilgrimage town at the edge of Pamban Island. Its location, close to the chain of shoals often associated with the Ramayana, has long been part of its identity.

On the night of December 22–23, 1964, a powerful cyclone struck the region. Storm surges moved across the low-lying land. A passenger train approaching the station was overtaken by the waves. By morning, much of the town had been destroyed. The event led to significant loss of life, and the area was later declared unfit for permanent habitation.

Remains of the railway station, church, and other structures still stand, marking the memory of what occurred.

This event highlights a broader consideration. *Certain locations carry recurring environmental risks* — coastal zones exposed to storm surges, regions along fault lines, areas shaped by long-term geological processes. Over extended periods, such places may experience events that reflect these underlying conditions.

In this sense, what may appear sudden often has deeper context. Not a fixed schedule, but a pattern shaped by natural forces over time.

"Preplanned," then, need not imply intention. It may point instead to the regularity with which natural systems operate within their own laws.

• • •

Tangshan, July 1976

In the early hours of July 28, 1976, a powerful earthquake struck the city of Tangshan in northern China. The shock came at 3:42 AM, when most of the city of one million people was asleep. By the time the second shock arrived in the afternoon, the city had already been almost entirely destroyed. Official figures place the death toll at 242,000. Independent estimates run considerably higher.

What makes Tangshan worth noticing in this chapter is what was reported in the days before.

Animals had been behaving strangely throughout the region for almost a week. Chickens refused to enter their coops. Cattle bolted from their pens. Mice and rats appeared in the streets in unusual numbers, moving in the same direction. Fish leapt out of ponds. Goldfish in domestic aquariums swam in repeated agitated circles. Pigs climbed walls. Some of these reports were noted by trained personnel; others by ordinary residents. A few were forwarded to local authorities.

The previous year, in 1975, a similar pattern of animal restlessness in nearby Haicheng had contributed to a successful evacuation, with relatively few casualties when the earthquake came. But by 1976, official scepticism had grown about whether the Haicheng prediction had been more luck than science. *The Tangshan signs were not acted upon.*

This is the difficult part of the chapter's observation. The signals were present. They were observed. They were even, in places, recognised. *What was missing was the willingness, in the system that received them, to take them seriously.* The animals did their work. The systems built to receive their report did not.

It is worth holding this case carefully. Not as a moral judgement, but as a sober record. What animals offer in the form of restlessness, what indigenous communities offer in the form of memory, what individuals occasionally offer in the form of unease before something happens — each of these is, in its own way, a signal. *Whether the signal is heard is a separate question.*

• • •

The Moral Question, Honestly

Pompeii is often presented as a moral example: a city of excess, followed by sudden destruction. The narrative appears simple. Yet the historical record suggests a more complex picture.

The region had already experienced a significant earthquake in 62 CE, years before the eruption of Vesuvius. Structural damage was visible, and the landscape had shown signs of instability. Some residents left. Many remained and rebuilt. The eventual eruption, while catastrophic, occurred within a setting where warning signs had already been present.

A similar complexity appears in accounts associated with ancient cities such as Sodom and Gomorrah. Archaeological work in the region has explored the possibility of sudden, high-temperature events — potentially linked to natural causes such as airbursts or other large-scale disruptions. Interpretations vary, and the relationship between physical events and later textual narratives remains a subject of ongoing study.

What emerges across these cases is a recurring pattern. Disasters occur. Over time, physical explanations may fade or become less clear. In their place, societies often construct moral interpretations to make sense of what happened.

These interpretations are not necessarily without value. They can reflect broader concerns about human behaviour and social stability. At the same time, the individuals affected by such events are not easily explained by simple moral categories.

A more grounded observation may be this: *natural systems operate without regard to human intention, while human societies sometimes increase their own exposure to risk through where and how they build.*

Disaster, in many cases, reflects the meeting of underlying conditions with visible events. *The lesson, then, may lie less in assigning guilt and more in recognising patterns before they become unavoidable.*

• • •

The Rare Understanding

Animals appear to respond because they remain closely attuned to the sensory capacities they possess. Communities such as the Moken or the people of Simeulue retain awareness through the transmission of knowledge across generations. In other traditions, long-preserved stories suggest that memory itself can function as a form of attention.

The question, then, may not be whether signals exist, but *how they are perceived* — and whether the means of perception have been maintained.

Modern life has placed increasing reliance on instruments. This has brought significant advances. Early warning systems, for example, now save lives that might once have been lost. At the same time, these systems depend on extended chains — measurement, communication, trust, and response. *Each link must hold for the system to function.*

Earlier forms of awareness were often more immediate — rooted in direct observation, environment, and shared memory. They were not infallible, but they operated differently.

• • •

A Note on What This Chapter Is Not Saying

This chapter does not suggest that disasters are moral punishments. It does not claim that those affected by them are at fault. It does not propose that belief or practice can prevent natural events.

It is making a narrower observation. *That environmental changes often produce signals before major events. That some animals appear to respond to such changes. That certain human communities have retained ways of recognising them. And that, in many cases, modern life has shifted attention away from these forms of awareness.*

It also suggests that traditional stories may preserve memories of past events — sometimes with a degree of correspondence to environmental changes, even when later interpretations have framed them differently.

These accounts are not merely dismissible. *They may carry traces of observation, shaped and transmitted across time.*

• • •

Accounts suggest that animals respond through sensitivity to their surroundings.
Human systems respond through structures we have built.
Both reflect ways of engaging with the same world.

The question is not why human cannot sense the nature,
but how to retain the discerning skills to be attentive.

CHAPTER TEN

Spiritual and Intellectual Protection

Awareness, Discernment, and the Inner Defence of Mind

Protection cannot be installed.
It is cultivated, layer by layer, across a life — through vigilant awareness and discernment.

The practices developed throughout this volume form the basis of that cultivation. They are how consciousness is nurtured and sharpened.

For it is the mind through which everything gains meaning.

• • •

What Is Being Protected

Before protection can be described, it is necessary to clarify what is being protected. Much popular writing assumes this is self-evident, focusing on techniques without first defining the object under threat.

It is not self-evident. *Protection is usually discussed only after disturbance appears, yet protection is often removed long before the disturbance is recognised.* The first assault may not fall upon the body, but upon the mind — upon feeling, attention, peace, confidence, discernment, or inner stability. What produces happiness, calmness, fear, confusion, temptation, or unrest is not always visible outwardly. Something within first loses balance before the outer life begins to reflect it.

What we call a person appears to consist of multiple layers. The body is one layer. The mind is another. The soul is understood as yet another dimension of human existence. Beyond these are the capacities through which human experience is received and interpreted: the attention of the senses, the perception of the mind, the discerning faculty, the talents that shape skills, inner strength that sustains endurance, and physical strength that sustains action. Through these gateways, influences are received, interpreted, accepted, resisted, or ignored.

Some aspects appear deeply individual. Others extend outward into relationships, environments, conversations, atmospheres, and systems of influence. *Human beings do not exist in isolation.* They are constantly interacting with words, emotions, ideas, pressures, memories, desires, and unseen forms of persuasion that shape both thought and behaviour.

Not every thought strengthens the mind. An excess of conflicting thoughts, pressures, and inward burdens may gradually disturb the balance of a person.

For it is the mind through which everything gains meaning.

The clearest demonstration of what is meant by inner protection comes, paradoxically, from a setting in which all outer protection had been removed.

In 1942, the Viennese psychiatrist Viktor Frankl was taken with his family first to the Theresienstadt camp, and from there to Auschwitz. He was thirty-seven years old. His wife, his parents, and his brother all perished. Of all that he had owned in his life as a doctor and a husband, only one thing was not taken from him: a single page of notes for a book he had been writing. That too was eventually destroyed.

What survived was something Frankl would later describe with some precision. In the worst hours of the camp, when men around him gave up and died within days, Frankl noticed that *something within him had remained intact.* It was not his body, which was wasting. It was not his identity as a doctor, which had been stripped. It was not his memory of his wife, which the guards could interrupt at will. It was something quieter and harder to name. *An inner observer. A small, lit candle of attention that the camp had not been able to reach.*

He used the word *space. Between stimulus and response,* he later wrote, *there is a space. In that space is our power to choose our response. In our response lies our growth and our freedom.* He had, in the worst conditions a human being can be placed in, found that the space was still there. Everything else had been taken. The space had not.

After his liberation he wrote *Man's Search for Meaning* in nine days, and went on to develop the school of therapy he called *logotherapy.* The book has remained in print for almost eighty years. What he was offering, in the language available to a twentieth-century psychiatrist, was a witness to the fact that *the inner space the chapter is describing is real— because it survived where almost nothing else did.*

The protection this chapter is naming is not theoretical. It has been demonstrated, under conditions that no theory could have predicted it would survive.

For this reason, protection cannot be understood merely as physical safety. *Intellectual protection* concerns the guarding of thought, judgement, discernment, memory, attention, and reasoning. *Spiritual protection* concerns the preservation of inward clarity, moral direction, inner peace, and the ability to discern what enters the inner world of a person. Before one can speak of spiritual warfare, mental resilience, temptation, deception, manipulation, or influence, one must first ask a more basic question: *What exactly within the human being is being protected — and how does that protection gradually weaken?*

Protection, if it is to be meaningful, must address more than one layer of human existence. Protecting the body alone preserves survival. For this reason, humanity has developed extensive systems of medical care, observation, diagnosis, and treatment to preserve physical health and respond to bodily danger. These are necessary and valuable. Yet survival alone does not always guarantee inward well-being, clarity, peace, or stability.

Protecting the mind requires a different form of vigilance. It demands awareness within one's own consciousness — the ability to observe thoughts, pressures, fears, influences, and inward conflicts before they gradually shape behaviour and perception. *To guard the mind, one must first attempt to identify the causes that disturb it.* This is one of the central purposes toward which this book gradually leads the reader.

Such inward work cannot be postponed merely for moments of spare time or occasional reflection. Discernment requires attentiveness during the ordinary movements of life itself — while speaking, listening, reacting, deciding, desiring, fearing, entertaining or thinking. *The urgency lies in the fact that disturbances often begin quietly before they are outwardly recognised.*

Consider an ordinary example. A person who has borrowed money knows that repayment is expected yet lacks the funds to return it. Before meeting the creditor, the debtor may repeatedly think within himself: *I hope he does not ask today. Perhaps he may come another time.* Such inward repetition may continue for days or weeks. Whether through hesitation, emotional tension, altered behaviour, avoidance, or subtle changes in interaction, the relationship itself may gradually begin to shift. The creditor may unexpectedly lose interest in asking immediately, delay the conversation, or feel reluctant to press the matter. Situations like these are often interpreted merely as coincidence, mood, psychology, persuasion, social pressure, emotional influence, or something more subtle operating within human interaction. Whatever explanation one prefers, the example illustrates how repeated inward movements of thought may quietly influence outward behaviour and relationships before they are consciously recognised.

Let us presume, for the sake of reflection, that words possess a kind of magnetic influence within human interaction — what the author provisionally describes as the *Electromagnetic Force of Words*. Through repetition, persuasion, fear, suggestion, emotional intensity, authority, symbolism, or collective influence, words may sometimes appear to shape attention, behaviour, emotion, and perception far beyond their immediate sound.

This is the third coinage the reader will meet under the small banner of the school of thoughts from which this book is written. It is offered here, as the others were, with the older inheritance acknowledged — the rabbis and prophets who spoke of words that build worlds, the desert fathers who watched suggestions arrive like spores carried on the wind, the Sufi teachers who held that words enter the heart at a different speed than they enter the ear, and the modern advertisers and propagandists who have studied the same effect with calculating precision and often without conscience.

What the *Electromagnetic Force of Words* names is the observed fact that *certain words — particularly when repeated, when emotionally charged, when delivered with authority, or when carried by a speaker the listener already trusts — appear to operate at a different level of force than ordinary speech.* They penetrate further. They remain longer. They subtly reorganise the inner field of the listener in ways the listener does not always notice and rarely consents to.

The author has come to use the word *electromagnetic* not to make a physics claim, but to mark the lawful, almost-measurable quality of this phenomenon. Like an electromagnetic field, the influence is invisible. Like an electromagnetic field, it operates whether or not the receiver is paying attention. Like an electromagnetic field, it can magnetise small filings of thought and align them, gradually, in a direction the receiver did not choose.

Where the inherited words still fit, they will be used as found. Where they bend, a new term will be coined, the elder house credited, and the difference stated in plain English. This is the third such coinage the reader has now met.

Some may interpret such influence psychologically, socially, spiritually, neurologically, or symbolically. Others may associate similar mechanisms with persuasion in advertising, crowd psychology, manipulative speech, ideological conditioning, ritual practices, occult traditions, or systems of influence built upon repeated suggestion and emotional reinforcement.

Whether understood literally, metaphorically, spiritually, philosophically, or psychologically, the importance of discernment remains central. *Not every recurring thought deserves acceptance.* Some thoughts strengthen clarity, while others may gradually weaken balance, peace, judgement, confidence, or inward stability. For this reason, attentiveness toward recurring thoughts becomes important. One may ask: *Why has this thought appeared repeatedly? Why now? What influence does it produce? Does it strengthen discernment, or diminish it?*

If inward disturbances become overwhelming, persistent, fearful, compulsive, or emotionally destabilising, one should not remain isolated. Wise counsel, trusted mentors, spiritual guidance, psychological support, or professional medical assistance may become necessary depending upon the situation. *Awareness should not produce fear, but vigilance.* The intention of this discussion is not to create paranoia, but to encourage attentiveness toward the influences that shape the inner life of a person.

This discussion becomes important because protection is not needed only during moments of crisis or visible disturbance. *Even a sound and stable mind requires vigilance.* Human beings now live within a world of constant movement, noise, persuasion, urgency, pressure, information, and emotional demand. The mind is seldom left entirely untouched. Thoughts continuously interact with conversations, media, memories, ambitions, fears, disappointments, desires, and the expectations of others.

For this reason, many people seek silence, distance, solitude, nature, prayer, retreat, or peaceful surroundings in an attempt to recover inward balance. Whether in a quiet field, a distant hillside, or a moment of stillness away from the demands of life, the human mind appears to search naturally for spaces of restoration. Yet even there, discernment remains necessary, *for protection is not merely the absence of noise, but the continued awareness of what shapes the inner world of a person.*

Every memorable book continues to live within the reader through its words. Certain words, ideas, stories, warnings, and reflections remain within memory long after the reading has ended. Some books entertain, some disturb, some persuade, some inspire, and some silently shape perception itself. For this reason, attentiveness toward words becomes important, because *words do not merely pass through the mind — they may continue interacting with it long afterward.*

Other forms of awareness that appear weak or under-developed may often depend upon the sharpness, balance, and discernment of the mind itself. For this reason, focusing only on one dimension — whether physical, mental, or spiritual — may eventually create imbalance within the person.

A more complete approach recognises the need for *coherence across these layers.* The discerning life depends upon this balance.

• • •

The Layers of Protection

This chapter does not attempt to provide an exhaustive system covering every field of physical, psychological, environmental, or spiritual protection, for vast volumes already exist on such subjects. The concern of this book is more specific: *the protection of mind, body, and spirit through inward vigilance and discernment.* Throughout these discussions, one central pattern repeatedly emerges — the importance of remaining alert within the movements of one's own mind.

Thoughts, fears, desires, imaginations, attractions, disturbances, interests, emotional reactions, and recurring inward impressions are often first experienced within consciousness before they become visible outwardly. Whether one encounters a conversation, an advertisement, an emotional atmosphere, a persuasive personality, a temptation, a fear, or even a disturbing environment, *the entrance of observation remains inward.* The outer world may present influences, but the inward response occurs within the mind. In this sense, the mind becomes the immediate field of discernment through which human experience is interpreted.

Even when observing the actions, words, inventions, or behaviours of others, one is still encountering the outward expression of another mind at work. Every product, argument, persuasion, system, performance, conflict, ideology, or artistic creation first begins within thought before appearing outwardly in the world. For this reason, *vigilance cannot be delegated entirely to institutions, systems, traditions, or external protections.* The inward door of discernment remains personal. One may receive guidance from mentors, physicians, spiritual teachers, counsellors, books, traditions, or communities, yet the responsibility of inward attentiveness ultimately remains within the individual.

Bodily protection remains necessary because the body sustains the conditions through which thought, attention, endurance, and action operate. Exhaustion, illness, addiction, neglect, or prolonged strain upon the body may gradually weaken clarity, emotional steadiness, and discernment. For this reason, adequate rest, nourishment, movement, and medical care remain valuable forms of protection. Yet bodily care alone does not necessarily preserve inward balance.

Mental protection concerns the quality of what repeatedly enters attention. Human beings now live amid continuous streams of information, persuasion, stimulation, comparison, urgency, and emotional influence. Not every thought deserves prolonged attention, and not every influence strengthens the mind. Certain forms of media, repeated fears, manipulative conversations, compulsive thinking, or continual inward conflict may gradually weaken peace, judgement, confidence, or clarity. *Discernment therefore involves learning to observe recurring patterns of thought without immediately surrendering to them.*

Spiritual protection concerns the preservation of inward steadiness, reflection, moral awareness, silence, prayerfulness, discernment, and the ability to examine oneself honestly. Whether through prayer, meditation, reflection, sacred reading, silence, contemplation, or other inward disciplines, many traditions have recognised the importance of guarding the inner life of the person. Such practices are not separated entirely from the mind, but often seek to strengthen attentiveness toward it.

These layers are not isolated from one another. Disturbance in one may gradually affect the others. Yet throughout them all, *the mind repeatedly appears as the meeting place where influences are received, interpreted, resisted, feared, accepted, magnified, or released.* For this reason, the discerning life begins not merely with outward defence, but with inward awareness.

• • •

How to Begin

By this point, the process has already begun. The practices introduced in earlier chapters are themselves forms of protection. Curtailment, evening reflection, the movement from mindnullness to mindfulness, attention to bodily signals, and the use of proportion as a diagnostic — all contribute to it.

What this chapter adds is structure. *These practices are not separate techniques, but parts of a coordinated way of living.* What may have been done in fragments can now be brought together.

The starting point is simple observation. Over the course of a week, notice where strength is already present and where it is not. Observe which environments support clarity and which diminish it. Notice which interactions leave a sense of steadiness and which do not. Attend to bodily signals, and begin to distinguish between those that require attention and those that do not.

By the end of this period, a pattern begins to emerge. Without deliberate effort, *a personal map takes shape* — showing where protection is functioning well and where it is less established.

The next step follows naturally. What is already strong is maintained. What is weaker is gradually strengthened. The work proceeds from what has been seen.

There is a long history of this kind of inward vigilance, practised not only in extremity but as a *daily discipline of ordinary life.*

The Roman Emperor Marcus Aurelius, who governed the largest empire on earth in the second century, kept a private notebook in which he wrote, almost daily, brief reflections to himself on what was passing through his mind. He was not writing for publication. The book — known to us as the *Meditations* — was found among his papers after his death. What it reveals is that *the most powerful man in the world spent the early hours of every day in inward observation*: testing his thoughts before they shaped his decisions, naming the impressions that had formed in him overnight, reminding himself of the principles he wished to preserve. Every morning, with no army to enforce it and no audience to watch, he placed his mind under quiet inspection.

He was not unusual in this. The ancient world, before the modern split between the religious and the secular, treated philosophy itself as a set of *spiritual exercises*, as the modern scholar Pierre Hadot has carefully shown. Stoic, Epicurean, Platonist, Pythagorean schools all taught daily practices of attention, perception, and judgement — less as theory than as inward technology, the means by which a mind was kept its own.

What this chapter names as the practices of protection is not a modern invention. It is the recovery of something the ancient world held as basic to a serious life. *The instruments existed. They were used by emperors, slaves, and shopkeepers alike. They were one of the things the ancient world taught its children.*

• • •

The Closing Argument

A natural question arises at this point: *are these practices sufficient?*

The honest answer is that no single approach is sufficient in every circumstance. Human life is complex, and situations arise that exceed preparation. *This is not failure. It is part of the condition we live within.*

The value of these practices lies in their range. They address much of what is encountered in ordinary experience. And *much* is not small. Over time, the difference between being protected in many situations and in none becomes significant.

This is not discouragement. It is clarity. *The work matters because it changes the quality of lived experience.*

There are also moments when what is required goes beyond personal effort. In such moments, support may come from sources not fully within one's control — through other people, through circumstance, through forms of understanding or strength that arise when needed.

The practices do not guarantee outcomes. *They prepare the ground.* They keep attention clear, and they make one more able to respond, receive, and remain steady.

• • •

Attend to what is within your care.
Remain open to what is beyond it.
Both are needed.
Neither alone is sufficient.

CHAPTER ELEVEN

Why Certain Places Disturb Us

Some spaces feel tense the moment we enter them.
Others seem to ease the body.

Often, this shift is noticed before it is understood.
The body responds before the mind forms an explanation.

This chapter explores the kind of attention that allows such responses to be observed more clearly.

• • •

Opening — Vigilant Silence

There are places that prompt an immediate impulse to leave, even before a reason can be named.

There are also places where the opposite occurs — where the shoulders settle, the breath deepens, and a sense of ease appears without any obvious cause.

In both cases, *the response arrives before deliberate thought.* The body registers something. Interpretation follows later.

Often, these reactions are attributed to visible factors — lighting, sound, smell, or the presence of others. These may indeed play a role. At the same time, there are moments when the source of the response is less easily defined.

This chapter introduces the idea of *vigilant silence*. Not silence as the absence of speech, but as a form of attention — a quieting of immediate interpretation so that experience can be observed more directly.

With this kind of attention, differences between environments become easier to notice. Some settings support steadiness. Others seem to unsettle it.

The practice is to observe these responses carefully, without rushing to conclusion.

• • •

Section I — The Architecture of Perception

The Animal and the Human

The previous chapter described how animals sometimes respond to changes that humans do not readily notice — movements inland, hesitation at thresholds, shifts in behaviour before events unfold. These responses need not be seen as extraordinary. *They may reflect differences in sensitivity and attention.*

Animals remain closely attuned to their surroundings. They respond to signals — vibrations, sounds, chemical changes — without the layers of interpretation that often accompany human perception.

Humans possess many of the same sensory capacities. *What differs is how those capacities are used.* Modern environments, routines, and patterns of attention can reduce sensitivity to subtle changes. Over time, perception may become more focused on what is immediately useful, while other signals receive less notice.

This section is offered as an exploration of that difference. Not as a recovery of something lost, but as a gradual re-engagement with ways of noticing that may have become less prominent.

• • •

The Blind Man and the Redistribution of Perception

Those who have spent time with individuals who lose their sight later in life often notice a shift. Hearing may become more refined. Touch becomes more attentive. Spatial awareness and sensitivity to tone or mood in conversation can appear heightened.

Research has explored this phenomenon. When visual input is reduced, the brain adapts by allocating more processing capacity to other forms of perception. *The senses themselves are not new, but their use becomes more pronounced.*

This illustrates an important principle. Perception is not only a matter of what senses are available, but how attention and processing are distributed among them.

When one channel dominates, others may receive less attention. When that dominance is reduced, previously underused capacities can become more noticeable.

In this sense, the practice described in this chapter is not about acquiring new abilities, but about *allowing existing forms of perception to become clearer.*

The discerning life, in this framing, involves learning to quiet dominant streams of attention — so that other forms of awareness can be observed more carefully.

• • •

Lashley and the Unlocated Memory

This volume has already referred to Karl Spencer Lashley, the American psychologist who spent decades searching for a single, precise location of memory in the brain and did not find one. His work suggested that *memory is not confined to a single point, but distributed across neural systems.*

Seen from this perspective, an important question arises: *how is memory organised, and how is it accessed?*

One interpretation is that memory is not stored as a fixed object in a single place, but as patterns distributed across networks — patterns that are reactivated rather than retrieved from a specific location.

Some have also explored broader ways of thinking about this process, suggesting that memory and perception may involve interaction between the brain and its wider context — environmental, relational, and experiential. These interpretations remain areas of inquiry rather than settled conclusions.

A similar question can be asked about perception. The brain processes incoming signals, but *what is perceived depends on how those signals are filtered, interpreted, and attended to*. Different individuals, in different conditions, may notice different aspects of the same environment.

This helps explain why the same place can be experienced differently by different people. The variation does not necessarily imply that the place changes, but that perception is shaped by attention, prior experience, and present condition.

The work of discernment, in this context, involves refining attention — *becoming more aware of how perception is formed, and how it may be sharpened over time.*

• • •

Darkness and the Sharpening of the Other Senses

There is a simple experiment that can be tried. Sit, for a short period, in a room that is fully dark — no screens, no external light. Remain still, and notice what changes.

As vision recedes, other forms of perception often become more noticeable. Sounds that were previously overlooked begin to stand out — the hum of appliances, distant movement, the rhythm of breath, the subtle shifts within the room.

Attention to the body may also increase. The temperature of the air, the movement across the skin, the contact with surfaces — details that were present but unnoticed can come into clearer awareness.

With continued stillness, internal sensations may become more apparent: breathing patterns, small areas of tension, the steady rhythm of the body's activity.

These changes do not introduce new senses. *They reveal activity that was already present.* When one channel dominates, others tend to recede. When that dominance is reduced, the balance shifts.

Darkness is one way of creating this shift. Silence can have a similar effect for sound. Stillness can do the same for movement. The principle is consistent: *when dominant inputs are reduced, other forms of perception become easier to notice.*

• • •

Silence

In this chapter, silence is not simply the absence of sound. *It is a condition of attention* — one in which the mind is less occupied with its own activity and more open to what is present.

Much of daily life involves continuous generation. Speaking sustains internal dialogue. Reading carries an inner voice. Planning projects attention into what is not yet here. Each of these has its place, but each also occupies the space in which quieter forms of perception might otherwise appear.

The cultivation of silence involves, at times, reducing this activity. Periods of not speaking. Stepping back from constant reading. Allowing planning to pause. Even brief intervals can create a noticeable shift. *When activity quiets, other forms of awareness may become more apparent.*

Many contemplative traditions have approached this in different ways, emphasising the value of stillness and attentive presence. What matters here is not the framework, but the experience itself.

Understanding the idea is a beginning. *The effect comes through practice.*

• • •

Section II — Places That Remember

The Gentler Residue

Certain places seem to carry a particular quality shaped by what has taken place within them. Earlier traditions referred to this as *the spirit of the place.* While the phrase has often been set aside, the underlying observation continues to be noted.

A library long used for focused study may feel different from one that is rarely used. A place of worship where people have gathered regularly may evoke a distinct atmosphere. A kitchen that has hosted years of shared meals, or a classroom shaped by a dedicated teacher, can leave a particular impression on those who enter.

There is a famous twentieth-century example of a person who deliberately set out to test this observation across forty years of his life.

In 1923, the Swiss psychiatrist Carl Jung began to build, with his own hands, a small round stone tower on the upper shore of Lake Zürich at a place called Bollingen. He laid each stone himself. There was no electricity. There was no telephone. There was no running water for many years. He cooked on a wood stove. He drew his water from the lake. Whenever life in the city had become too much, he came to Bollingen and placed himself within the stones he had laid.

Over the next four decades he added a second tower, then a third, then a small courtyard. Late in life he carved figures into the stones — inscriptions in Latin and Greek, images he had received in dreams. He wrote, near the end of his memoir, that the tower had become *a confession in stone*. He found, increasingly, that he could not write or think well anywhere else. The place itself, he said, had begun to think with him. *He could feel it remembering what he had brought to it across the years.*

Jung was not a sentimental man, and he was not a religious one in any conventional sense. He was a careful clinical observer who had spent his entire professional life watching what happened in the inner lives of his patients. The tower at Bollingen was, for him, a long experiment in the question this chapter is asking. *Can a place hold the residue of what has happened within it?* Jung's answer, after forty years of personal observation, was yes — quietly, unmistakably, yes.

The tower still stands. It is not open to the public. The current generation of his family lives there, and they have reported — cautiously, and not for general audience — that the quality Jung had described continues to be felt by those who enter it.

These impressions are not attributable to a single factor. Architecture, use, memory, and expectation all play a role. Over time, repeated patterns of activity can shape how a place is experienced.

In some environments, this experience is supportive. Focus may come more easily. A sense of steadiness may be present. In others, the opposite may occur — restlessness, unease, or distraction.

The practice here is not to assume a cause, but to notice the effect. Some places appear to support clarity and engagement. Others seem to make them more difficult.

With experience, these differences can be recognised more readily. Where possible, *time can be directed toward environments that support what one is trying to do, and limited in those that do not.*

• • •

Objects of Long and Intimate Use

A similar observation is sometimes made with objects, though on a smaller scale.

Objects used over long periods, especially with care and consistency, can feel different from those that are new. A ring worn for decades may carry a sense of familiarity. A book read daily over many years may feel distinct from a newly printed copy. Tools shaped by repeated use often seem more *settled* in the hand than identical ones just acquired.

There is a particular puzzle in the world of music that illustrates this observation more sharply than any other example.

Antonio Stradivari, a violin maker in Cremona, Italy, produced approximately six hundred instruments between 1666 and his death in 1737. Roughly five hundred and fifty of them survive. They are now among the most valuable objects on earth — the finest examples sell for sixteen to twenty million dollars at auction. A single violin made by Stradivari is widely regarded as producing a quality of sound that no later instrument has been able to reproduce.

This is not a sentimental judgement. It has been tested. For more than a century, scientists, luthiers, and acoustic engineers have attempted to discover what makes a Stradivarius sound the way it does. The wood has been analysed under spectrometers. The varnish has been chemically reverse-engineered. Modern violins have been built to Stradivari's exact dimensions, with wood from the same Alpine forests, with varnishes matched to the chemistry of the originals. *They do not sound the same.*

In recent years, a possibility has been quietly raised in the research literature. The wood of a Stradivarius has, over three centuries, been continuously vibrated by master players — hours every day, year upon year, generation upon generation. The cellulose structure of the wood, it is now thought, has been gradually altered by this prolonged sympathetic vibration. The instrument has, in a sense, *been played into being*. The hands that have held it have left something in it that no laboratory can shortcut.

This is, of course, only one current hypothesis. The full answer remains unsettled. But the basic fact stands: *an object that has been used continuously, attentively, and at the highest level of human skill for three hundred years has become something that an identical new object is not.* The chapter's observation about objects of long and intimate use has, in the world's most carefully studied instruments, an unusually clear demonstration.

These impressions may arise from multiple factors — wear, memory, association, and personal meaning. Over time, repeated interaction between a person and an object can shape how that object is experienced.

This helps explain why certain objects are valued beyond their material form. Heirlooms often carry significance because of their history of use and the relationships associated with them. In many traditions, objects intended for regular or meaningful use are handled with care, *reflecting an awareness of this continuity.*

At times, people also report that objects from different contexts seem to evoke different responses. Whether this is due to memory, association, or expectation, the experience itself is worth noticing.

For objects that will be used over long periods, attention to how they are handled can influence the relationship that develops with them. Over time, familiarity and use can shape how they are perceived and experienced.

• • •

The Body as First Reporter

One of the most immediate ways of sensing a place is through the body. As noted earlier, *bodily responses often arise before conscious interpretation.*

On entering a space, a brief pause can reveal subtle changes. The shoulders, the breath, the abdomen, the jaw — small shifts may be noticed without effort. These responses occur quickly and continue as long as one remains in the environment.

A sense of tension or ease may appear. These reactions can be influenced by many factors — surroundings, prior experience, expectation, or current state. *Rather than assigning a cause immediately, the useful step is to notice the response itself.*

With practice, these signals become easier to recognise. The body provides information consistently; what changes is the degree of attention given to it.

There is one twentieth-century story that demonstrates what can happen when a person learns, through long necessity, to listen to the body's signals as their primary instrument.

Gladys Aylward was an English parlourmaid with no theological training and almost no money, who, in 1932, paid her own way to a remote mountain region of northern China to work as a missionary. She was small, plain-spoken, and stubborn. She did not speak Mandarin when she arrived. She learned the local dialect in the first year by walking among villagers and listening with her whole body to how they used their words.

In 1940, with the Japanese army advancing through Shanxi province, the local prison and orphanage where she had worked for eight years were threatened. The children would not survive an occupation. Gladys, then thirty-eight years old and weighing barely one hundred pounds, gathered one hundred children — many of them under the age of seven — and led them on foot across the Taihang mountains toward the Yellow River and safety beyond. The journey took twenty-seven days. They walked through territory occupied by Japanese soldiers, with no map, no escort, and only the food and water they could find on the way.

Years later, in interviews and in her own quiet account, Gladys was asked how she had chosen the route. She said something the listeners did not quite know what to do with. *She had not chosen by reasoning,* she said. *Many times, when she came to a fork or a ridge, the body had simply told her which way to go.* A heaviness on one path. A lightness on the other. She had learned, over the eight years before, to trust this. The children had survived. So had she.

The story was later dramatised in *The Inn of the Sixth Happiness* (1958). The original Aylward record, in the writings of those who interviewed her, is more sober and in some ways more remarkable than the film. *She had become an instrument so finely tuned to the difference between safe and unsafe ground that the body could read it before the mind had words for it.* This is the faculty the chapter is naming — demonstrated, not in a meditation room, but on a mountain path, with one hundred children and an army behind.

The faculty is not extraordinary. It is ordinary, in the sense that it belongs to every body that has been allowed to develop it. *What is extraordinary is what the faculty becomes when a life is staked on listening to it.*

The difference lies not in whether signals are present, but in *whether they are observed.*

• • •

The Challenger's Error

A common question arises: *if such differences in experience exist, why are they not noticed by everyone — especially by those who are attentive and analytically trained?*

The question is reasonable.

One possible response is that attention can be directed in different ways. Analytical and verbal modes of attention are highly developed in many forms of training. These modes are effective for reasoning, explanation, and argument. *They are not always the same as the forms of attention involved in noticing subtle bodily or environmental responses.*

The kinds of observations described in this chapter tend to arise in quieter forms of attention — through bodily awareness, stillness, and the suspension of immediate interpretation. These are not unfamiliar capacities, but they may be less emphasised in some contexts.

This is not a criticism. *It reflects differences in focus.* Where one mode is developed, another may receive less attention.

The approach suggested here is simple. Rather than accepting or rejecting the claims, they can be explored through direct experience. The experiments described earlier — time in quiet, attention to bodily responses, comparison across environments — provide a way of testing the observations personally.

No belief is required. Only attention, applied in a different way.

• • •

What Is Missing Is Not the Data

A possible conclusion emerges from the observations in this chapter.

The question may not be whether information is present, but *how it is noticed.* Environments, objects, and bodily responses all provide signals — some obvious, some subtle. *These signals are not always absent; they are often overlooked.*

What is less consistent is the reception. Attention may be directed elsewhere — toward thought, interpretation, or ongoing activity. In such cases, quieter forms of perception receive less notice.

The work described in this chapter is the cultivation of that reception. Through practice, attention can become more sensitive to what is already present. Over time, this sensitivity may begin to feel natural rather than effortful.

In this sense, *discernment is not an added layer, but a refinement of awareness.* It involves noticing more clearly, without needing to name everything immediately.

• • •

Some places feel different.

Some objects carry associations shaped by their use.

Some responses arise more readily in some conditions than others.

The discerning life pays attention to these differences.

And then continues — quietly — with what has been noticed

CHAPTER TWELVE

Why Powerful Words Clear What Advice Cannot Move

Many people engage deeply with ideas yet find that their patterns remain largely unchanged.

Information can be understood, even appreciated, without producing lasting transformation.

• • •

The Reader Who Has Read Too Many Books

There is a familiar pattern among those who spend time with self-improvement material. They are thoughtful, engaged, and genuinely interested in change. They read widely, take notes, attend discussions, and explore multiple approaches.

Yet over time, the underlying patterns of life may remain similar. *Effort is present, input is substantial, but the results do not always match the intention.*

This chapter explores why that gap can occur.

One possible explanation is that information operates at one level, while the patterns that sustain behaviour operate at another. *Understanding alone may not reach the level where change is formed.*

It is like watering the surface of soil that does not easily absorb. The water is present, but it does not reach where it would be needed.

Advice can guide and encourage. But change often requires something that engages more directly with the structures that hold patterns in place.

• • •

Kahneman's Honesty and Its Limit

Daniel Kahneman, the Nobel laureate, near the end of his career offered a formula for success that was honest enough to make many readers uncomfortable.

Success = Talent + Luck.

And, for great success, Kahneman added, the formula becomes:

Success = Talent + a Great Deal of Luck.

The honesty of this is striking. Kahneman, the most careful observer of the cognitive errors humans make, was telling readers that the great successes they admire are largely the products of factors the successful person did not earn.

The honesty is admirable. The formula is also incomplete.

It is incomplete because it leaves out two factors that the careful observer can verify across thousands of lives. It leaves out the *relentless effort* that the talented person, having received their talent, did or did not apply. And it leaves out the *discernment* with which the effort was directed.

The reader has met talented people who applied themselves and went nowhere. The reader has met talented people who applied themselves with discernment and went very far. *The luck factor cannot account for the difference.* Something else is operating. The Beaugrun framework names it.

Success = Skilfulness + Hard Working +
Application of Prudence.

And luck — Kahneman's luck — is the *complimentary gift*, given to some practitioners by the field they have been operating in. Luck completes the formula. *Luck does not constitute it.* The practitioner who has the three components and receives luck on top is the practitioner the world calls a great success. The practitioner who has the three components and does not receive luck is also successful; in ways the world does not always notice but which the discerning observer can see.

Kahneman saw clearly. He was honest about what he saw. The chapter offers the addition that completes what he had honestly described. *The luck was the part Kahneman could measure. The other three were the parts that lay beneath measurement, and which the careful observer of life can recognise even when no instrument has registered them.*

• • •

The Adidas Repositioning

An example from marketing helps illustrate the distinction between information and influence.

In the early development of athletic footwear, advertising often focused on features. Shoes were described in terms of materials, durability, and construction. These claims were accurate and informative, and they supported steady but limited engagement.

Over time, the messaging shifted. Brands such as Adidas and Nike began to emphasise a different approach. Rather than describing the product alone, their campaigns spoke to identity and aspiration. Phrases like *Impossible is Nothing* or *Just Do It* did not explain the shoe. They addressed *how the wearer might see themselves.*

This shift coincided with significant changes in how audiences responded. While many factors contribute to such outcomes, the difference in messaging highlights an important point: *communication that connects with identity and motivation can have a different impact than communication that presents information alone.*

This example is not offered as endorsement, but as illustration. The same product can be received differently depending on how it is framed.

The chapter's focus is not on marketing itself, but on what this distinction suggests. *When change is required, information may not always be sufficient. Something that engages more directly with motivation and identity can sometimes reach where information alone does not.*

• • •

Why Advice Fails

Advice often falls short for structural reasons that are worth examining.

It is typically received at the level of conscious thought. It is understood, evaluated, and sometimes stored for later use. *Yet understanding and storing do not necessarily lead to change.*

Many patterns of behaviour are sustained by processes that are not fully conscious — habits, emotional responses, and repeated associations built over time. These do not always shift simply because new information has been introduced.

As a result, knowing what to do and doing it can remain separate. The understanding is present, but the underlying pattern continues.

This helps explain a familiar experience: *effort is sincere, insight is gained, yet change is limited.* The issue is not a lack of intelligence or intention. It is that different aspects of experience are being engaged at different levels.

For change to occur, the engagement often needs to reach beyond explanation alone — toward the patterns that shape response more directly.

• • •

What Powerful Words Are

Powerful words are different from advice in their structure. *They are not propositions to be evaluated. They are utterances that operate in the layer where the operating happens.*

A proverb is closer to a powerful word than an article. A scripture verse, received deeply, is closer to a powerful word than a sermon's exposition of it. A line of poetry that has stayed with the reader for years is closer to a powerful word than a paragraph of analysis explaining what the line means. *The shorter forms reach lower into the person than the longer forms can.* The shorter forms have been compressed. *The compression is what allows them to move past the conscious mind's evaluation and into the layer that operates beneath.*

This is also why every careful spiritual tradition has placed enormous weight on short formulations that are repeated. The *Jesus prayer* in the Christian tradition. The *mantras* of the Hindu and Buddhist traditions. The *Shahada* in the Islamic tradition. The *Shema* in the Jewish tradition. Each is a short, repeated formulation that, over years of repetition, reshapes the practitioner at a layer that conceptual instruction could not reach.

There is one historical example of this principle developed with such precision that it deserves a closer look, because it is essentially the chapter's technique demonstrated in a fourth-century laboratory.

Around the year 380, in the deserts of Egypt, a former Constantinople deacon named Evagrius Ponticus settled in a small community of monks at a place called Kellia. He had been one of the most brilliant young theologians of his generation. He gave it all up to spend the rest of his life in a stone cell, watching what happened in his own mind.

Across two decades, Evagrius did something no one had done before. He systematically catalogued the recurring intrusive thoughts that arrived in the practitioner's mind — not in the abstract, but as he himself observed them, hour by hour, year by year. He named eight categories: gluttony, lust, greed, sadness, anger, listlessness, vainglory, and pride.

(These eight, refined by Pope Gregory the Great two centuries later, would become known to the Western world as *the seven deadly sins.*) But Evagrius's purpose was not classification. *His purpose was to find a way to interrupt them.*

And here was his method. For each pattern of intrusive thought, he selected a single short verse from scripture — sometimes only five or six words — to be spoken back to the thought at the moment it arrived. Not as argument. Not as theology. *As interruption.* He gathered these into a treatise of more than five hundred such verses, which he called the *Antirrhētikos* — in Greek, *the speaking-back.*

Evagrius had observed something the modern reader is in a position to verify in their own experience. *Long argument with an intrusive thought strengthens the thought.* The act of reasoning with it engages it at the level on which it operates. But a short, settled, well-chosen utterance, returned to repeatedly without elaboration, *interrupts the thought at a layer the thought cannot defend.* This is precisely what the chapter is now naming. The form is fifteen hundred years older than the chapter. The technique is the same.

The desert fathers were not theorists. They were observers, in the same sense that this volume has been observation. They were testing, on themselves, what worked. Their five-hundred-verse handbook is one of the earliest pieces of evidence that the chapter's claim is sound.

The powerful word is not magic. *The powerful word is the form that words must take in order to operate at the depth where reshaping happens.* The depth is real. The forms that reach it are particular. The reader who has spent years receiving advice without change is not failing. *The reader has been using forms that do not reach the depth.* The chapter is offering the reader the forms that do.

• • •

How Powerful Words Clear

The effect of powerful words can be described, even if the description does not fully capture the experience.

When a phrase is repeated over time, especially in a settled state of attention, it can begin to influence how thoughts and responses are organised. *The change is usually gradual.* Early repetitions may seem to have little effect, while continued practice can make the phrase more familiar, more available, and more integrated into daily awareness.

The influence is not only in the meaning of the words, though meaning plays a role. It also appears to lie in *repetition* and *the condition in which the repetition occurs.* When attention is steady and less distracted, the phrase can be received differently than when it is repeated mechanically.

These two elements — repetition and attentiveness — work together. Either can have some effect on its own, but their combination often proves more noticeable over time.

There is a more recent demonstration of this principle that the modern reader has likely heard of, in distorted form, without knowing the original.

In the early 1900s, a French pharmacist named Émile Coué, working in Nancy in eastern France, observed something curious in his shop. The patients to whom he gave a particular medicine, while quietly assuring them it would help, recovered more reliably than the patients to whom he gave the same medicine without the assurance. Coué was not interested in deception. He was interested in what was actually operating.

Across the next twenty years he developed a careful method, which he called *autosuggestion.* The patient was asked to repeat, twenty times each morning on waking and twenty times each evening on falling asleep, a single short phrase: *Day by day, in every way, I am getting better and better.* The phrase was always the same. The repetition was always the same. The state of attention — the threshold of sleep at one end, the threshold of waking at the other — was specifically chosen because Coué had observed that *the layer where reshaping happens is more reachable in those moments than in fully waking thought.*

By the early 1920s his clinics were treating many thousands of patients annually. The reported clinical improvements — of conditions ranging from chronic pain to certain forms of depression to several stubborn physical complaints — were dramatic enough to draw public attention across Europe and North America. The medical establishment, unable to explain the results within its theoretical framework, was largely embarrassed by them. Some doctors absorbed elements of the method into their own practice without crediting Coué. Others dismissed the entire phenomenon as suggestion. *The phenomenon was suggestion. That was Coué's point.*

The phrase has long since drifted into popular culture in adulterated form, often quoted with mild mockery. The original protocol — the precise count, the precise moments of the day, the precise calm of repetition without reasoning — has rarely been told properly to a modern reader. Coué had, in his small French pharmacy, recovered the same essential technique that Evagrius had developed in the desert and that the great spiritual traditions had carried for thousands of years. *Short phrase. Steady repetition. Settled attention. The reshaping that follows.*

Many traditions have made use of established phrases that have been repeated across generations. Such phrases may be easier to adopt because they are already structured for memorability and repetition. At the same time, individuals may also find meaning in phrases that resonate personally.

The key is not the origin alone, but the *continuity of practice.* Over time, repetition in a receptive state can influence how experience is shaped and responded to.

• • •

The Practice

The practice offered here is simple in form and gradual in effect.

Choose a short phrase that holds meaning for you. It may come from a tradition you follow, or from one you respect. It should be brief enough to repeat easily and clear enough that you are comfortable returning to it.

Set aside a short period each day — around ten minutes. Sit in a quiet place and allow the body to settle. Begin repeating the phrase, either silently or softly. Let the repetition continue for the duration of the time.

There is no need to create a particular feeling or result. *The practice is not evaluative.* It is a repetition carried out with steady attention.

When the time ends, stop and return to the day without analysis.

Continue this regularly over a period of weeks. After some time, you may begin to notice whether anything has shifted. The change, if it comes, may be subtle or gradual.

If the practice feels meaningful, it can be continued over longer periods. Over time, repetition may become more natural, and the phrase more familiar within everyday thought.

The effect is not immediate. It develops through consistency.

• • •

Closing

The reader who has read this far, and who has perhaps recognised themselves in the description of the reader who has read everything and changed nothing, is now in a position to do something different.

The volume has been advice in some places. The chapter has been advice. *Advice has its uses. The volume does not dismiss it.* But advice is not the layer at which what the volume has been pointing toward is finally received.

The final reception happens through the practices. *The reading of the volume is the preparation. The practices are the operation.* The reader who reads without practising has received the preparation and not done the operation. The reader who practises without reading might receive the operation without the preparation, but the operation is sometimes harder to begin without the preparation that the reading provides.

The volume is offered to be read. The practices are offered to be done. *Both, together, are what the volume is for.*

• • •

Advice motivates. It does not activate.

Powerful words activate.

They reach the layer where reshaping actually happens.

And the practitioner, after years of repetition, becomes the reshaping.

PART IV

Capacity, Talent, Innocence

What is in You, and What Has Been Waiting to Come Forward

13. Are Talents and Skills Biological or Spiritual?

14. Innocence Teaches Perception Better Than Science

CHAPTER THIRTEEN

Are Talents and Skills Biological or Spiritual? How Do They Become Inactive?

Where Talent Comes From — and Where It Goes

The prodigies the standard account cannot predict.
The capacities that arrive in some practitioners
after years of clearing.
The talent that is not absent but obstructed.
This chapter offers an architecture honest about all three layers.

• • •

The Question No One Has Asked Honestly

Where does talent come from?

Common explanations are well established: genetic predisposition, environment, opportunity, and sustained practice. The interaction of these factors accounts for much of what we observe in the development of skill.

These explanations are meaningful and supported by evidence. They describe many pathways through which ability is formed and refined.

At the same time, certain cases invite further reflection. There are individuals who display advanced abilities at unusually early ages — musical, mathematical, linguistic, or artistic. These instances are often described as exceptional or rare, and they are typically understood within the same framework as intensified versions of familiar processes.

The most carefully documented case in the historical record is the one the standard account most struggles with.

Wolfgang Amadeus Mozart was born in Salzburg in 1756. By the age of three, he was picking out chords on his older sister's harpsichord. By the age of four, he was reproducing entire pieces after a single hearing. By the age of five, he had begun to *compose.* The earliest of his surviving compositions — a small Andante and an Allegro for keyboard, catalogued as K. 1a and K. 1b — were written down in his father's hand, with the date *January 1761* noted in the margin. The boy who dictated them was four years and eleven months old.

By eight, Mozart had written his first symphony. By twelve, he had completed his first opera. He never had what would today be called a music education in the formal sense; his father, a competent court musician, simply could not keep up with him after the first few years.

The standard account of talent — genetic predisposition, environmental opportunity, ten thousand hours of deliberate practice — explains a great deal of what humans do. *It does not explain Mozart at five.* The deliberate practice had not yet had time to occur. The genes are not enough; his sister Nannerl, who shared them and trained alongside him, was a fine pianist but never composed at his level. Something else was operating. The chapter does not pretend to know what. It only points out that the standard account knows it does not know either, and has, for the most part, declined to say so plainly.

Mozart is the most famous case of a phenomenon that is not actually rare. Every generation produces a small number of children whose abilities arrive *before* the conditions the standard account requires. The question this chapter is willing to ask is not what such children inherit, but *what such children are receiving — and from where.*

Whether the existing framework fully accounts for such cases remains open to interpretation. The examples suggest that the range of human capacity may be broader than commonly described, and that not all variation is easily anticipated.

This chapter does not reject existing explanations. It considers whether they might be part of a larger picture — one that includes not only how abilities are developed, but *how they appear, remain unused, or become more visible over time.*

• • •

The Standard Account and Where It Strains

A widely accepted view is that talent reflects biological capacity shaped through environment and practice. Genetic predispositions, developmental conditions, and sustained effort together contribute to the skills we observe.

This framework explains a great deal. It accounts for family patterns of ability, cultural concentrations of skill, and the importance of timing and training in development. *It remains an essential part of understanding how talent appears and grows.*

At the same time, certain cases invite further consideration. Early prodigies, individuals with highly uneven abilities, and accounts from artists and practitioners describing moments of unexpected clarity or insight all point to experiences that are not always easily predicted.

These examples do not invalidate the standard account, but they suggest that it may not fully capture the range of how talent is experienced. In many descriptions of creative or skilled work, individuals speak of moments that *feel less constructed and more received* — where the outcome seems to exceed what deliberate effort alone would have produced.

One way to approach this is to consider that biological and environmental factors prepare the conditions under which ability develops, while leaving open the question of *how certain expressions of that ability arise.*

This chapter explores that question, not by replacing existing explanations, but by considering whether they might be part of a broader picture.

• • •

The Architecture of Capacity

This chapter proposes a way of looking at capacity across multiple dimensions — *biological, experiential, and what may be called the receptive.*

The *biological layer* refers to the physical and neurological characteristics a person is born with. Differences in sensory systems, motor coordination, and cognitive processing are well documented. These variations influence how easily certain skills can be developed and how far they may be extended.

The *experiential layer* reflects what is done with those capacities. Practice, instruction, repetition, and sustained engagement all contribute to the development of skill. This layer has been widely studied and remains central to understanding performance.

Alongside these, there is another way in which some individuals describe their experience. In creative and highly skilled work, people often report moments that feel less constructed and more *discovered* — where outcomes seem to arise with a sense of ease or unexpected clarity.

There is a famous account of this kind of receiving from someone whose credentials were beyond doubt.

Henri Poincaré, the French mathematician of the late nineteenth century — a figure of the same stature in mathematics that Einstein would later occupy in physics — wrote a careful description of how some of his most important discoveries had actually come to him. He had been working for weeks on a particular problem in mathematics, the theory of what he called *Fuchsian functions*. The work had gone nowhere. He had set the problem aside and gone with his geological excursion to Coutances. As he was stepping onto the omnibus to leave the town, with his mind on entirely other matters, *the solution arrived.* It arrived complete. It arrived with such immediate certainty that he did not feel the need to verify it. He continued his conversation with the friend he was travelling with. He wrote the solution down later, at his ease, and on checking it found it correct.

Poincaré published this account in 1908, in his book *Science and Method.* He was not given to mystical claims. He was, on the contrary, one of the most rigorous mathematical minds of his century. He had simply observed, in his own work, that *the most important parts of his discoveries had arrived in moments when he was not consciously working on them*. The conscious work prepared the ground. *The arrival itself was something else.*

Poincaré was not alone. Friedrich Kekulé reported that the ring structure of benzene came to him in a daydream of a snake biting its tail. Sir William Rowan Hamilton said the equations of quaternions arrived as he was crossing the Brougham Bridge in Dublin, and he carved them into the stone of the bridge with his pocket-knife on the spot. Many writers have reported the same with their best lines.

The chapter is not claiming these arrivals are mystical. It is observing only what every careful practitioner across many fields has observed: *that the most important moments of creative work do not feel constructed but received.* The standard account treats these moments as a curious by-product of unconscious processing. The chapter is asking whether the reception itself is part of the architecture of capacity, and not merely an artefact of how a busy brain consolidates its work overnight.

This can be approached as a difference in how individuals access and organise their abilities. Some configurations of attention, sensitivity, and training may allow for patterns or insights to emerge more readily than others.

From this perspective, capacity may involve not only what is built through practice, but also *how effectively a person is able to notice, integrate, and express what becomes available to them.*

This does not replace the biological or experiential accounts. *It offers a third lens* for considering how certain forms of ability appear and develop over time.

• • •

How Channels Become Obstructed

A natural question follows: *if ability depends on multiple factors, why does it sometimes remain unexpressed?*

One possibility is that the capacity is *not absent, but constrained or underdeveloped.*

These constraints can take different forms. Some are *biological* — differences in physical or cognitive systems that influence how easily certain abilities can emerge. These are real and, in many cases, set practical boundaries. Within them, adaptation and alternative pathways remain important.

Others are *developmental or experiential.* Early environments may not support emerging abilities. Educational systems may favour certain forms of expression over others. Family or social dynamics can discourage or redirect what begins to appear. These influences can shape whether a capacity is strengthened, redirected, or left unused.

There are also *internal patterns* — habits of attention, emotional responses, and learned ways of interpreting experience — that can limit how abilities are accessed or expressed. These patterns are not fixed. Over time, they can be recognised and gradually adjusted.

There is a category of clinical case that puts the chapter's claim in particularly sharp relief, because it overturns the standard architecture of how talent is supposed to work.

Kim Peek, born in 1951 in Salt Lake City, was the man on whose life the film *Rain Man* was based. He had been born without the *corpus callosum* — the thick band of nerve fibres that, in most brains, connects the left and right hemispheres. At fifty years of age he could not button his own shirt, dress himself without help, or perform many tasks that a six-year-old performs without thought. *And yet.* Kim Peek could read two pages of a book simultaneously, one with each eye, in roughly ten seconds. He retained, by his neurologists' careful estimates, about ninety-eight percent of what he read. By the end of his life he had memorised the contents of approximately *twelve thousand books* — every page of every one of them — along with the entire road system of the United States, the calendars of the past several centuries, and the complete classical music repertoire.

Kim Peek had not built these abilities through practice. *They had been there from the beginning.* His brain, in being assembled differently from the standard arrangement, had — in some way that the neuroscience of his lifetime could only partly describe — *opened a channel that the standard arrangement keeps closed.*

There is a related and even more startling category. *Acquired Savant Syndrome.* In the medical literature, there are now over fifty documented cases of ordinary adults who, after a head injury or a stroke or a particular kind of brain illness, suddenly find themselves able to do things they had never been able to do before. A man struck on the head by a wave at a Mexican beach woke as a mathematical savant, capable of drawing complex geometric patterns he had no training to understand. A boy hit by a baseball developed perfect pitch and an instant grasp of musical composition.

A woman after a stroke began to paint, with no instruction, in the manner of accomplished oil painters.

The standard account of how talent develops cannot accommodate these cases. *The talent was not built. It was, in some sense, released by an obstruction or a rearrangement of what had been blocking it.* The capacity, the cases suggest, had been there all along. What the injury did was not to install something new. What the injury did was to *remove what had been preventing the existing capacity from coming through.*

This is precisely what this chapter has been pointing toward. Not that all human ability follows this pattern — most does not. But that *the cases at the edge of the standard account suggest the architecture is more layered than the standard account is willing to say.*

Different kinds of limitations call for different responses. Some involve adaptation. Others involve learning, practice, or supportive guidance. Still others may respond to changes in attention and habit.

From this perspective, the absence of visible talent does not always indicate the absence of capacity. *In some cases, it reflects conditions that have not yet allowed that capacity to become visible.*

Change, when it occurs, tends to be gradual and shaped by the conditions in which a person continues to work.

• • •

The Hopeful Implications

Taken together, these observations suggest a possibility worth considering.

The range of a person's ability may not always be fully reflected in what they have experienced so far. *In some cases, capacities that have not appeared may not be absent, but unexpressed or limited by conditions that have shaped their development.*

If those conditions change — through practice, attention, or different forms of engagement — new aspects of ability may begin to emerge. This does not imply that all limits can be overcome. Biological factors and individual differences remain significant.

At the same time, it allows for a more open view of potential. *Some assumptions about what a person cannot do may be based on past circumstances rather than fixed capacity.*

There are many instances of individuals developing new skills or deepening existing ones later in life, sometimes in ways they had not anticipated earlier. These changes are often gradual and depend on sustained effort and favourable conditions.

The implication is not a guarantee, but an invitation: *to consider that ability may be broader than it has appeared, and that under different conditions, aspects of it may become more visible.*

• • •

How to Begin the Clearing

The work described here is not separate from what the volume has already introduced. *The practices outlined in earlier chapters can be understood as contributing to a gradual process of change.*

The walkover from mindnullness to mindfulness, the careful handling of emotional responses through curtailment, the evening review and release of daily patterns, attention to bodily signals, the cultivation of inner protection, the recognition of how places and powerful words shape inner condition — *all of these influence how a person relates to their own experience.*

Over time, consistent engagement with these practices can reduce patterns that limit attention, expression, or engagement. The process is gradual and cumulative rather than immediate.

As conditions change, different capacities may become easier to access. *What emerges will not be the same for everyone, and it may not align with initial expectations.*

For this reason, the emphasis is not on targeting a specific ability, but on maintaining the practices themselves. Directing too much effort toward a particular outcome can sometimes create tension that works against the process.

A more sustainable approach is to continue the practices and observe what develops over time. *The direction of change may not be predictable, but it can still be meaningful.*

• • •

The Both-and Posture

Talent and skill can be understood through multiple perspectives. Biological factors play a role. Experience and practice also shape development. In addition, some descriptions of ability include moments that feel less constructed and more discovered, *suggesting another dimension to how capacity is experienced.*

Rather than choosing one explanation to the exclusion of others, a broader view allows these perspectives to be held together. Each highlights a different aspect of how ability forms and is expressed.

For those interested in developing their capacities, this suggests a balanced approach: *attending to physical and cognitive conditions, engaging in sustained practice, and remaining open to how ability may unfold in ways that are not fully predictable.*

This integrative stance — *holding more than one frame at once* — has been a recurring theme throughout the volume. It expands what can be noticed and allows for a more flexible understanding of what a person may be capable of.

• • •

Closing

The act of engaging with this chapter already reflects certain capacities — attention, reflection, and the willingness to consider unfamiliar ideas. *These are not trivial. They are part of how growth becomes possible.*

For those who have been applying the practices described in the volume, it is likely that some changes — however subtle — have already begun. These changes may not always be obvious, but they often accumulate over time.

The chapter leaves the reader with a possibility rather than a conclusion: *that ability may be broader than it has appeared, and that under different conditions, aspects of it may become more accessible.*

What emerges will vary from person to person. The process is gradual, and its direction is not always predictable.

• • •

Is talent biological or spiritual.

Talent is experiential.

Talent is also a channel through which something larger operates.

The channels can be obstructed.

The obstructions can be addressed.

And the capacities, when freed, sometimes return.

CHAPTER FOURTEEN

Innocence Teaches Perception Better Than Science

The four-year-old sees what the adult has been trained out of seeing.

The cultivated innocence of the practitioner adds the child's perception back to the adult's accumulated knowledge.

The combination is what the discerning life is finally for.

• • •

The Child Who Sees What the Adult Cannot

Young children sometimes observe aspects of a situation that adults may not immediately register.

A child entering a room may attend to small details — the positioning of objects, subtle shifts in tone between people, or changes in familiar surroundings. *These observations are not necessarily more accurate, but they are often less filtered.*

Adults, by contrast, tend to rely on established categories. These are useful — they support communication, decision-making, and efficient action. At the same time, they can narrow attention, guiding it toward what is expected and away from what is not.

The difference is not that one sees more and the other less, but that *attention is organised differently*. One is more immediate and open; the other is more structured and selective.

Human development involves learning how to interpret the world through shared frameworks. This process is necessary. It allows individuals to function within complex environments.

At the same time, it raises a question: *whether some of the openness of early perception can be retained — or consciously revisited — without losing the benefits of developed understanding.*

This chapter explores that possibility.

• • •

What Has Been Trained Out

It is helpful to be specific about how perception shifts over time.

Awareness of bodily signals can become less immediate. Children often respond quickly to hunger, fatigue, or emotional states. Adults, influenced by schedules and expectations, may become less attentive to these signals until they are more pronounced.

Sensitivity to the emotional tone of others can also change. Children sometimes respond to nonverbal cues — tone, posture, atmosphere — before words are fully processed. Adults, accustomed to focusing on language and meaning, may rely more heavily on what is said than on how it is conveyed.

The experience of environments can shift as well. Early perception may include
a broad, impression-based response to a place, while later perception often emphasises identifiable features — size, function, or status.

Judgements about trust and intention can follow a similar pattern. Initial impressions may arise quickly, but social learning often encourages these impressions to be moderated or reconsidered in light of norms and expectations.

In each case, the change is not simply a loss. *It reflects a reorganisation of attention.* Certain forms of perception become less prominent as others become more structured and refined.

That such a reorganisation can be more than metaphor — that the *trained-out* perception can leave a measurable trace in the brain itself — became one of the most uncomfortable findings of late-twentieth-century neuroscience.

In December 1989, the regime of Nicolae Ceauşescu fell in Romania. International researchers entering the country in the months that followed found something they had not been prepared for. In state institutions across Bucharest and other cities, more than one hundred and seventy thousand children had been raised since infancy in conditions of profound neglect. They had been fed and clothed. *They had not been spoken to, looked at, or held.* Some had spent the first several years of their lives staring at the ceiling above their cribs, with no adult attention except the placement of bottles.

The Bucharest Early Intervention Project, beginning in 2000, followed a cohort of these children through childhood and into adolescence. The findings have entered the medical literature and have been carefully replicated. Compared with children placed early into foster care, the children left in the institutions showed *measurable reductions in the volume of the brain regions responsible for attention, perception, and emotional response.* The MRI scans showed it. The cognitive tests confirmed it. *What had not been received — the steady gaze of an adult, the ordinary tones of a kind voice — had not merely failed to develop. It had altered the brain that was supposed to develop it.*

This is the most uncomfortable kind of evidence the chapter could ask for. *What is trained out of children is not a metaphor.* It is, in extreme cases, visible on a scan. The chapter has been observing, gently, that adult perception has been reorganised away from the openness of early childhood. The Bucharest cohort is the part the science of the late twentieth century could not deny: *that the openness, when it is starved, leaves an absence that the body itself remembers.* The good news, also documented in the project, is that early intervention — the placement into a real family before the age of two — produced significant recovery. *What has been trained out can sometimes be trained back in. But it is the steady attention of a present adult that does the work.*

These shifts support participation in complex social and conceptual systems. At the same time, they may reduce the immediacy with which certain kinds of information are noticed.

The question the chapter raises is whether aspects of this earlier openness *can be brought back into awareness*, alongside the understanding that develops over time.

• • •

The Son Who Did Not Cry

There is a personal observation that may help illustrate the chapter's theme.

When the author's son was born, there was a brief moment in which the baby did not cry immediately. The medical staff, attentive to normal indicators of newborn health, watched closely. Crying is commonly understood as an important sign of respiratory adjustment, and its absence, even briefly, can draw concern.

In that moment, the father held the child and wondered — quietly — about the experience from the child's perspective. *Not as a medical question, but as a reflective one.*

The surrounding interpretations of birth are often shaped by established frameworks — biological, clinical, and cultural. These are essential and necessary. At the same time, they do not fully describe what the experience might feel like from within.

The brief stillness before the child began to cry became, in this instance, *a moment of reflection rather than alarm.* The cry came soon after, and the child's health was not in question. What remained was the impression of a transition — a shift from one state to another, observed in a small interval.

This account is offered not as an alternative explanation, but as an illustration of how perception can include *both interpretation and observation.* Even within well-understood processes, there may be moments that invite a different kind of attention.

The reader is not asked to adopt this view, only to consider that familiar events can sometimes be noticed in more than one way.

• • •

Innocence Is Not Naivety

A careful distinction is needed between *innocence* and *naivety*.

Naivety refers to a lack of awareness about how situations or people may operate. It reflects limited experience or information, and it can leave a person unprepared for complexity.

Innocence, as used in this chapter, points to something different. It refers to a quality of perception that remains relatively direct — less dominated by assumption, expectation, or habitual interpretation.

A person may be well-informed and experienced, and still retain moments of this kind of perception. *The difference lies not in what they know, but in how they attend.* Knowledge is present, but it does not fully override immediate observation.

The distinction the chapter is making here is one that the Indian contemplative tradition formalised many centuries ago, and the vocabulary it developed is precise enough to be useful.

The Sanskrit word *bhāvanā* — sometimes translated as *cultivation*, sometimes as *bringing into being* — refers to the deliberate practice of keeping a particular quality of attention alive. It is not naivety, which is the absence of training. It is also not knowledge, which is the accumulation of categories. *Bhāvanā is the careful gardener's work of keeping a clearing open in a forest that always grows back.* Without that work, the categories of adult interpretation grow over the clearing within a few years, and the direct perception that was natural to the four-year-old becomes inaccessible to the forty-year-old.

The yoga teacher T. Krishnamacharya, who taught throughout the first half of the twentieth century in southern India and whose students reshaped the modern global practice of yoga, observed something that the early visitors to his school often noted in passing. *The children of his oldest students retained, into their own adulthood, a quality of direct perception that their parents had spent decades trying to recover.* The parents had come to the practice as adults, with their categories already grown over. The children had been raised in households where the practice was simply how attention was held. *They had never lost what their parents were working to find.*

This is an old observation, in many cultures, by many names. The Christian desert fathers spoke of *katanyxis* — the heart kept tender enough to be moved. The Sufi tradition spoke of *fitra* — the original disposition, which can be obscured but never destroyed. The Buddhist tradition spoke of *shoshin* — *beginner's mind* — cultivated by the most experienced practitioners precisely because it was hardest to keep. *Each tradition observed the same thing. Each developed practices to preserve what the world's ordinary growing-over would otherwise have buried.*

Innocence, in the sense this chapter means it, is not the original condition that the child has. *It is the condition that the practitioner, by careful attention, has refused to let go of — or, having lost it, has slowly recovered.*

Many traditions have described this as a quality that can be cultivated. *It is not a return to childhood, but a way of holding awareness that allows both understanding and openness to coexist.*

The aim is not to become uninformed, but to remain attentive in a way that is not entirely shaped by prior conclusions.

The combination — *clarity of knowledge alongside openness of perception* — is what this chapter is exploring.

• • •

Why This Matters for the Discerning Life

The kind of awareness described throughout this volume depends on more than analysis alone. *It involves both observation and interpretation.*

Perception provides the initial contact with what is present. Reasoning helps to organise, evaluate, and understand what has been noticed. When either is emphasised without the other, the picture can become incomplete.

Some aspects of experience are not immediately accessible through reasoning alone. They are first registered as impressions, responses, or patterns that are then interpreted. *In this way, perception and reasoning work together rather than in opposition.*

This is why the theme of innocence appears at this stage. Earlier chapters have introduced frameworks, practices, and ways of observing. *This chapter highlights the quality of attention through which those tools are used.*

The development of this kind of attention often involves a shift in how certainty is held. Strong reliance on established interpretations can sometimes narrow what is noticed. *A more open stance allows for observation before conclusion.*

This does not require abandoning knowledge, but holding it with flexibility. Over time, this balance can support a way of engaging with experience that is both informed and attentive.

The change is gradual. *It develops through continued practice and reflection.*

• • •

The Practice

The practice offered here is simple in form and gradual in effect.

Once a day, set aside a short period — around ten minutes. Sit in a quiet place and allow the body to settle. During this time, attend to what is in front of you with fresh attention, *as if encountering it without relying immediately on familiar labels.*

This is more challenging than it sounds. The mind naturally identifies and categorises what it sees. The aim is not to stop this process entirely, but to *notice it and gently return to direct observation.*

Attention may shift between naming and noticing. Each time this happens, the practice is simply to come back to looking — to shapes, textures, movement, and presence.

With repetition, moments of less structured attention may become more frequent. *These moments do not replace understanding, but they sit alongside it.*

Over time, this can support a way of perceiving that includes both familiarity and openness. What is known remains available, but it does not fully determine what is seen.

This is one way of approaching the quality described in this chapter — *not a return to an earlier stage, but an adjustment in how attention is held.*

• • •

The Vigilance That Does Not Sleep

There is one further point that must be made before this volume closes, because without it the reader may misunderstand what the entire book has been pointing toward.

The practices described in these pages — the ten minutes of repetition, the evening review, the body scan, the period of silence, the patient observation of recurring thought — are doors. *They are not the room.* The room is the rest of the day. The room is the conversation with the colleague at noon, the message that arrives at three o'clock and asks for a quick reply, the friend who calls in the evening and says something that lingers, the voice on the radio that uses certain words instead of others, the meeting that ends with a decision that has somehow been made for everyone in the room before any of them knew they had agreed to it.

The discerning life is not an activity scheduled for a particular time. It is the quality of attention with which all other times are inhabited.

The reader who has reached this final chapter has been preparing for a long shift in how the ordinary day is held. The morning practice opens the door. *What walks through the door is the rest of the day.* The vigilance that the volume has been describing is not the vigilance of the meditation cushion, useful as that is. It is the vigilance that does not sleep — the steady inner observer who watches the thought arrive, watches the word come from another's mouth, watches the body's small report of unease at the threshold of a particular room, watches what the field of speech is asking the listener to consent to before the listener has noticed there is a question.

This is the work that the chapters of this volume have been quietly preparing the reader to take up. The volume ends here. *The work, for the reader who chooses it, begins here.*

And this is also why the book belongs to a series. There is more to be said. The next volumes will take up specific terrains — the chemistry of relationships, the long arithmetic of inheritance, the work of cultivating a household that does not undo what has been built in the morning, the question of what to do when the field one is operating in is itself disturbed. The work of the school is not the work of one volume. *This volume has been the door.*

The reader who has come this far has earned the right to walk through it.

• • •

Closing

This chapter appears at the end of the volume because it returns to a central theme: *the role of perception in how experience is understood and lived.*

The ideas presented throughout have offered ways of thinking and observing. The practices have suggested ways of engaging with them. Together, they point toward a shift in how attention is directed.

For some readers, the value may lie in the frameworks. For others, in the practices. For others still, in the gradual changes that come from applying them over time.

Any shift that occurs is likely to be gradual rather than dramatic. It may take the form of small changes in how situations are noticed, how responses are shaped, and how understanding develops.

Over time, attention may become quieter and more stable. What was once effortful may become more natural. *What is noticed may expand, without needing to be named immediately.*

This is one possible direction the volume has been exploring. *What follows from here depends on how each reader continues.*

• • •

The child sees what the adult cannot.
The trained mind has displaced the perception.

The perception can be recovered, slowly, in the mind of the adult.
The recovery starts from giving up pride.

And the discerning life, in its mature form, walks silently
with what has been recovered.

Afterword

• • •

You have reached the last page.

But the journey does not end here.

Check your mood. Compare it to where you began. Something has shifted — however quietly. *The changes you have noticed may have happened when something that had been operating within you stepped out — quietly, without announcement.* Be alert in discerning your body experiences. They may return with power.

The Kingdom of Spirits surrounds us. *We are living among them.* They appear as words. Suddenly, you may feel it. You glance behind you, beside you — sensing a presence. Somebody nearby. Unseen. There you are. *The Words are Spirits, and they are alive.* Discern every word that comes to you. And you are now more equipped to listen to your heart. Practice makes perfection.

• • •

If at any point after reading you feel distressed, disturbed, or overwhelmed — with a feeling that the same moods you had earlier have returned — *speak with a trusted mentor, your family doctor, or a qualified therapist.* These experiences deserve proper human support — not silence.
Walk forward with awareness. With prudence. With an open heart.

— *Beaugrun*

A Few Words to Carry

from Beaugrun School of Thoughts

• • •

Thinking is not merely the interaction of neurochemicals.
Thinking is talking to something within one selves.

...

Every word that comes to you has a motive.
Never ignore inner words.

...

The brain is not where memory lives.
The brain is the door through which memory enters.

...

Mindnullness is the disguise. Mindfulness is the unveiling.
The walkover is a lifelong journey. Be attentive to maintain the pace.

...

Patterns form through repetition. Notice what you allow to continue.

...

The body reports before the mind analyses. Discern its experiences carefully.

...

Advice motivates. It does not activate.
Power behind the words activate.

...

Recovery starts where pride is identified.

...

A Questionnaire

for Self-Reflection

• • •

These questions are for your personal awareness only. They are not a diagnostic test. They have no scoring. They have no right or wrong answers. *They are an instrument of attention* — questions designed to direct your noticing toward what the volume has been pointing at, in the form of your own life.

Sit somewhere quiet. Take your time with each question. The first answer that arrives may not be the truest answer. Allow the question to operate in you for a few moments before you consider it answered. Some questions will produce immediate, clear responses. Others will produce silence at first, and then, hours or days later, a recognition that the question had been operating in you all along.

Both kinds of response are useful. Neither is a failure of the practice.

If any response stirs deep disturbance, confusion, or prolonged distress — *please speak with a trusted mentor, family doctor, or qualified therapist.* These questions are designed to open attention, not to substitute for human support where human support is needed.

• • •

1. ***Have you had an experience of hearing the words of a loved one who is no more?***

The experience may have been a single sentence, a familiar phrase, a remembered tone of voice, or simply the unmistakable sense that they had spoken even when no audible words were present. *Notice the quality of the experience.* Notice when it occurred. Notice what was happening in you, and around you, in the moments before.

2. ***Did that experience bring you comfort — or disturbance?***

This question matters more than the previous one. *The presence is not, by itself, the diagnostic. The quality of what the presence carried is.* Comfort suggests one source. Disturbance suggests another. Mixed feelings — which are common — suggest layers worth attending to with the practices the volume has been teaching.

3. ***Do you find certain words or phrases returning to your mind repeatedly without obvious reason?***

These returning words may be praise, accusation, instruction, threat, encouragement, or something whose category is not immediately clear. They may be in the voice of someone you know, or in a voice you cannot identify. *The recurrence is the data.* Notice the words. Notice the conditions under which they return. Notice whether their return is connected to any pattern in your day or your life.

4. ***Have you noticed a connection between those recurring words and your mood or behaviour?***

The connection, if it exists, may be subtle. The words may arrive shortly before the mood shifts. The mood may persist as long as the words are operating and recede when the words recede. The behaviour that follows may be one you would not have chosen if the words had not been present. *The chain the volume's chapter on curtailment described may be visible, in your own life, when this question is held with patience.*

5. ***Do you experience unexplained sadness, restlessness, or sleeplessness without an identifiable cause?***

Notice the disproportion. The sadness that exceeds the visible occasion. The restlessness in the evening when the day was peaceful. The sleeplessness in a quiet bedroom when the body is tired. *These are the wet patches the volume has described.* Notice when they appear. Notice what preceded them. Notice whether the appearance is associated with particular places, particular conversations, particular times of the year.

6. ***Have you ever felt a presence near you that you could not explain?***

The presence may have been comforting or disturbing. It may have been familiar or foreign. It may have lasted seconds or hours. The presence is data. The quality of the presence is more data. *The dismissal of the presence — which most adults perform automatically — is itself worth noticing.* The dismissal is the trained adult mind operating. The presence preceded the dismissal.

7. ***Have you noticed your energy levels shift after certain conversations or environments?***

Some conversations leave you lifted. Others leave you depleted. Some rooms send you out heavier than you entered. Others send you out lighter. *Begin to notice which is which, in your own life.* Over weeks, the pattern, when it emerges, will give you information you can act on. The volume's chapter on places that disturb us describes what you may be reading.

8. ***Are there words spoken to you in childhood that still visit you today?***

The words may have been encouraging or wounding. They may have come from a parent, a teacher, a sibling, a stranger. *The visit they continue to make, decades later, is the report of something that was deposited at the time of the speaking and has continued to operate since.* The visit is not, by itself, harmful. The continued operation, unrecognised, sometimes is. Recognition is the beginning of attending to it.

9. ***Do you find it difficult to identify what you are feeling — or why?***

The difficulty is common. The trained adult mind has often been taught to override the body's reports in favour of the categories the surrounding culture provides. *The recovery of the capacity to identify what you are feeling is one of the recoveries the practices have been teaching.* The difficulty does not mean the feelings are not there. The difficulty means the channel through which the feelings would have been recognised has been narrowed. *The channel can be widened with patient practice.*

10. *After reading this book — has anything shifted in your awareness?*

The shift may be subtle. The shift may be substantial. The shift may not yet be visible to others. *The shift is for you to assess.* If something has shifted, the volume has done what the volume was for. If nothing has shifted, the volume may need to be returned to. Some readings reach the reader on the second visit, when the conditions for reception have changed since the first.

• • •

If your reflections raise deeper questions — *do not carry them alone.* Reach out to a trusted mentor, your family doctor, or a qualified therapist. *Seeking help is not weakness. It is wisdom.*

The questionnaire is not the end of the practice. *It is the doorway into the next stage of it.*

The Series Ahead

Why the Need of the Hour

• • •

You have just finished a book that was not supposed to exist.

Not because it could not be written. But because everything around you — every institution, every industry, every system of knowledge that governs modern life — has operated, consciously or otherwise, to ensure that what is written in these pages was rarely assembled in one place, rarely stated this plainly, and rarely placed in the hands of a reader.

And yet here it is. *And you have read it.*

• • •

The world is in crisis.

Not merely politically. Not merely economically. Not merely environmentally — though all of those crises are real and urgent.

The deepest crisis of this hour is a crisis of understanding.

Humanity does not know what it is.

It does not know what drives it. What wounds it. What heals it. What speaks to it in the night. What follows it through generations. What hides beneath the surface of every thought, every impulse, every memory, every fear.

It has been given answers — by science, by medicine, by law, by psychology, by the self-help industry, by institutions of every kind.

But the answers have not healed everything they were asked to heal.

Depression deepens. Addiction spreads. Mental illness multiplies. Medicines multiply without curing. Children inherit the wounds of grandparents they never met. And people pray — sincerely, desperately — without always knowing what they are praying against.

Something is being asked at the foundation. And a question at the foundation cannot be answered only at the surface.

• • •

This series exists because the hour invites it.

Not a series of spiritual encouragements. Not a collection of motivational insights dressed in scripture.

A careful, documented, patient inquiry.

Into the foundations that have been laid — in neuroscience, in psychiatry, in pharmacology, in law, in philosophy — upon which an entire civilisation has built its understanding of the human being.

And in the space the inquiry opens — a rebuilding.

Of what humanity actually is.

Of what actually drives it.

Of what actually heals it.

Of what it is actually facing.

And of how — finally, practically, urgently — to walk forward.

• • •

Each book in this series examines a different wall of the same structure.

Spirituality is Extremely Dangerous. Why? — the volume you have just finished. It names the territory and lifts the veil.

If Brain Has No Memory, How Does the Human System Work? — the volume that follows the scientific evidence to where the institution did not follow it.

And the books that follow — each one a different angle, a different discipline,
a different opening into the larger field of inquiry that the Beaugrun School of Thoughts has been mapping.

You do not need to read them in order. *You need to read the one that speaks to where you are.*

But by the time you have read them all — much may look different.

Your mind. Your memory. Your struggles. Your personality. Your prayers. The news. The prescription in your hand. *The voice you heard in the night that sounded exactly like someone you lost.*

• • •

This is the need of the hour.

Not more information. *Transformation of understanding.*

Because until humanity understands what it is actually engaging with, it will keep addressing the surface while the depth continues to operate undisturbed.

• • •

Let us crack all odds!

Not as a slogan.

As a decision.

Made here. Now.

With the volume you have just closed in your hand.

— *Beaugrun*

Glossary

of Beaugrun Terms

• • •

These are the principal terms developed within this volume, gathered for the reader's reference and for the future work of the school.

• • •

Mindnullness — *(Chapter 4)* The state in which attention has been emptied without awareness. The mind is awake but absent; thoughts pass without leaving a trace in conscious memory. Distinct from sleep, which is a clear absence, and from mindfulness, which is full presence.

Mindfulness (older sense) — *(Chapter 4)* The cultivated capacity to notice what is operating in oneself, with sufficient precision that the act of noticing begins to alter what is operating. Distinguished in this volume from the wellness-industry version. *Discernment, applied with care, to the inner life.*

The Walkover — *(Chapter 4)* The sustained practice by which a person moves from mindnullness to mindfulness, and the *pace* by which the movement is maintained.

Soulsology — *(Chapter 5)* The proposed branch of inquiry developed within the Beaugrun School of Thoughts. Where psychology describes the thought after it has arrived, Soulsology asks the prior question: *who or what is sending the thought to be received?* Not in conflict with psychology; working at a different depth of the same chain.

The Wet Patch — *(Chapter 5)* A disproportionate feeling whose visible cause does not account for its intensity. The chapter's guiding image:

water appearing on a shelf around an undisturbed vessel — evidence of a leak that lies elsewhere. *The wet patch is the report.*

Curtailment — *(Chapter 5)* The practice of attending to the chain *thought → feeling → bodily sign → emotion → behaviour* early enough that attention can interrupt its momentum. Distinct from suppression. *The feeling is not rejected. It is noticed and named.*

The Unseen Energy Link — *(Chapter 5)* The pattern by which a recurring trait may not be entirely the person's own, but the report of an energy that has been linking them to something else — a generational current, a place, or a particular relationship.

The Body as Antenna — *(Chapter 6)* The body's capacity to register changes before the conscious mind has formed an interpretation. *The first reporter is at work, in everyone, all the time. The question is only whether the reader has learned to read the report.*

The Body That Transmits — *(Chapter 6)* The complementary observation that the body is not only a receiver but a quiet broadcaster. The cardiac field extends measurably outward and influences nearby bodies; *the body sends in a band the older traditions called spirit.*

Newton's Flight Principle — *(Chapter 8)* The corrective to the popular reading of the boomerang effect. A word sent out as harm does not return as a counter-blow aimed at the sender. *The action did not provoke an opposite action; it provoked a flight.* Trust withdraws, goodwill flees, the field empties — and the speaker, having not stepped outside the field, is left living in the conditions the throw has produced. *The boomerang has not been thrown back at the thrower. The thrower has remained standing in the place where the throw was made.*

The Beaugrun Doorway — *(Chapter 8)* The pattern by which a single throw of word, act, or held thought returns over time as a long line of arrivals. Each current in the field responds in its own time, but the mind has only one doorway through which response can reach it. *The fortieth* *response may arrive a decade after the throw, by which time the thrower has long forgotten what was thrown.*

The Practice of the Evening — *(Chapter 8)* The brief evening review of the day's speech and held thought, with the inward release of what carried harm. Not erasure — the practice does not undo what was said — but the interruption of repetition.

The Beaugrun Position — *(Chapter 3)* The chemistry-and-spirit framework: *the body is chemistry; the trigger that produces chemistry comes from beyond chemistry; the spirit is the chemist; the body is the laboratory.*

Vigilant Silence — *(Chapter 11)* Not silence as the absence of speech, but silence as a *condition of attention* — a quieting of immediate interpretation so that experience can be observed more directly.

The Electromagnetic Force of Words — *(Chapter 10)* The observed fact that certain words — particularly when repeated, when emotionally charged, when delivered with authority, or when carried by a trusted speaker — operate at a different level of force than ordinary speech. They penetrate further, remain longer, and subtly reorganise the inner field of the listener. *Like an electromagnetic field, the influence is invisible. Like an electromagnetic field, it operates whether or not the receiver is paying attention.*

The Beaugrun Success Formula — *(Chapter 12)* The corrective to Kahneman's *Talent + Luck*. *Success = Skill + Hard Work + Prudence.* Luck is the complimentary gift, given to some practitioners by the field they have been operating in. Luck completes the formula. *Luck does not constitute it.*

The Powerful Word — *(Chapter 12)* The form a word must take to operate at the depth where reshaping happens — short, compressed, repeated, received in a settled state of attention. *Not a proposition to be evaluated, but an utterance that operates in the layer where the operating happens.*

The Receptive Layer — *(Chapter 13)* The third layer of the architecture of capacity, alongside the biological and the experiential. Names what every careful practitioner across many fields has reported: *the most important moments of creative work do not feel constructed, but received.*

The Vigilance That Does Not Sleep — *(Chapter 14)* The closing claim of the volume. *The discerning life is not an activity scheduled for a particular time. It is the quality of attention with which all other times are inhabited. Be alert always. Test everything.* The morning practice opens the door; what walks through the door is the rest of the day.

The Discerning Life — *(throughout the volume)* The way of living the entire volume has been preparing the reader to take up: a mind kept attentive within the ordinary movements of life, neither reacting nor withdrawing, but observing, naming, and choosing.

About the Author

• • •

Beaugrun is an independent observer and researcher of the spirit kingdom, with over three decades of sincere inquiry. Neither theologian nor psychologist — but a persistent truth-seeker and a lawyer who refused to dismiss what others labelled illusion.

He withdrew from nearly a decade of legal practice to develop and ground the framework presented in this volume. He is the founder of the *Beaugrun School of Thoughts* and the originator of *Soulsology* — the proposed science of the soul. He writes from Kerala, India.

This is his first published work in English. Further volumes of the Beaugrun School of Thoughts are in preparation, alongside the planned *Beaugrun Soulsology Research Journal.*

Beaugrun™ • *Soulsology*™ • *Beaugrun School of Thoughts*™

Beaugrun Soulsology Research Journal™

Detailed Contents

• • •

Front Matter

Dedication v

A Note to the Reader vii

A Word Before You Begin viii

Acknowledgements xi

Why I Write — A Note from the Author xiv

Part I — Foundations of Thought and Spirit

1. Thinking — A Conversation with Spirits 1

Opening the Pandora Box of Spirits World 2

It's Different 5

The Thinkers Without a Brain 5

Then What Is the Brain For? 7

The Footprints of Thought 8

The Spirit in the Particle 9

The Narrow Window 10

The Chain Unbroken 11

The Field You Are Standing In 12

2. If Brain Has No Memory, Mind Has No Power, And Body Has No Life — How Does a Human Function? 15

Why the Silence 15

The Fog That Will Not Lift 16

Let Us Crack the Iceberg of Mind 17

The Traditional Mindology 20

But First, Some Homework 21

3. **Let Us Do Some Chemistry of Spirits** 23

The Opening Innovation — God Is a Chemist 23

The Hierarchy 24

The Body as Chemistry 25

The Reverse Proposition 25

The Scriptural Anchors — Hell Fire, Hell Darkness 26

The Atomic Foundation 27

The Dark Matter Wondering 28

Death and Recombination 30

The Beaugrun Position 31

4. **A Walkover from Mindnullness to Mindfulness, and How to Maintain the Pace** 33

The Word Itself 33

How Do We Move from Mindnullness to Mindfulness? 35

The Effects Are Not the Cause 36

Places, Buildings, Premises 37

The Diagnostic by Contrast 37

The Wandering and the Trap 39

The Disguise of Autonomy 39

The Seduction Sequence 40

The Visible Sign 41

When the Spirit Steps Out 41

Maintaining the Pace 42

Part II — Diagnostics of Disturbance

5. **Curtail Feelings Before Emotions Conquer Behaviour** 45

The Vessel and the Wet Patch 46

The Reverse Approach 48

Two Vocabularies, One Sequence 49

The Body Reports Before the Mind Names 51

The Disguise 52

The Undercurrent of Waving and Patting Seems Unhealthy 52

The Practices 53

Curtailment Is Not Suppression 54

Personality Traits and the Unseen Energy Link 55

6. The Body Speaks Before the Mind Names 57

The Body as Antenna 57

The Body That Transmits 59

Signals Worth Noticing 60

Timing Is Diagnostic 61

Three Layers, Not One 62

Notice Without Obeying 63

A Caution 63

7. Memory Loss and Forgetfulness — A Chemical Analysis 65

The Puzzle of the Eminent Forgetful 65

What Science Has Established 66

Where the Standard Explanation Strains 66

Two Directions of Loosening 68

The Laughing Gas Comparison 69

Disturbance Is Not Deletion 70

The Place-Dependence Diagnostic 71

The Both-and Posture 73

Practical Discernment 73s

8. Hurt Not Others. It Returns. The Boomerang Effect 75

Words Carry Force 75

The Returning Motion 76

The Other Direction 78

The Practice of the Evening 79

What This Practice Does 80

A Caution 81

Part III — Discernment and Environment

9. Are Natural Disasters Preplanned? Animals Discern. Why Can't Humans? 85

The Elephants of Yala 85

The Small Science of What They Detect 87

What We Traded Away 88

Myth as Compressed Memory 89

Dhanushkodi, December 1964 90
Tangshan, July 1976 91
The Moral Question, Honestly 92
The Rare Understanding 93
A Note on What This Chapter Is Not Saying 94

10. Spiritual and Intellectual Protection — Awareness, Discernment and the Inner Defences of Mind 95
What Is Being Protected 95
The Layers of Protection 101
How to Begin 103
The Closing Argument 104

11. Why Certain Places Disturb Us 107
Opening — Vigilant Silence 107
***Section I** — The Architecture of Perception*
The Animal and the Human 108
The Blind Man and the Redistribution of Perception 109
Lashley and the Unlocated Memory 110
Darkness and the Sharpening of the Other Senses 111
Silence 111
***Section II** — Places That Remember*
The Gentler Residue 112
Objects of Long and Intimate Use 114
The Body as First Reporter 116
The Challenger's Error 117
What Is Missing Is Not the Data 118

12. Why Powerful Words Clear What Advice Cannot Move 119
The Reader Who Has Read Too Many Books 119
Kahneman's Honesty and Its Limit 120
Success = Skill + Hard Work + Prudence
The Adidas Repositioning 121
Why Advice Fails 122
What Powerful Words Are 123
How Powerful Words Clear 125
The Practice 127

Part IV — Capacity, Talent, Innocence

13. Are Talents and Skills Biological or Spiritual? 131
The Question No One Has Asked Honestly 131
The Standard Account and Where It Strains 133
The Architecture of Capacity 134
How Channels Become Obstructed 136
The Hopeful Implications 138
How to Begin the Clearing 139
The Both-and Posture 140

14. Innocence Teaches Perception Better Than Science 143
The Child Who Sees What the Adult Cannot 143
What Has Been Trained Out 144
The Son Who Did Not Cry 146
Innocence Is Not Naivety 147
Why This Matters for the Discerning Life 149
The Practice 149
The Vigilance That Does Not Sleep 150

Back Matter

Afterword 153
A Few Words to Carry 154
A Questionnaire for Self-Reflection 155
The Series Ahead — Why the Need of the Hour 159
Glossary of Beaugrun Terms 162
About the Author 166

www.ingramcontent.com/pod-product-compliance
Ingram Content Group UK Ltd.
Pitfield, Milton Keynes, MK11 3LW, UK
UKHW041351190726
13845UKWH00026B/547

9 789334 188592